The
Promise of
America

☆ ☆ ☆

The
Promise of
America

AN HISTORICAL INQUIRY

John Morton Blum

HOUGHTON MIFFLIN COMPANY BOSTON
THE RIVERSIDE PRESS CAMBRIDGE

1966

E
175
.9
.B63

First Printing w

AUTHOR'S NOTE

Chapter four of this book is adapted, with the permission of the Publishers, from my chapter, "The Public Image: Politics," pp. 134-153 of *American Perspectives*, edited by R. E. Spiller and Eric Larrabee, published by the Harvard University Press. Copyright © 1961 by The President and Fellows of Harvard College. I am also indebted to the President and Fellows of Harvard College for permission to quote from *The Letters of Theodore Roosevelt*, 8 vols. (Cambridge, 1951-1954), Harvard University Press.

Chapter five of this book is adapted, with the permission of the Publishers, from my chapter, "Exegesis of the Gospel of Work: Success and Satisfaction in Recent American Culture," pp. 17-36 of *Trends in Modern American Society*, edited by Clarence Morris, published by the University of Pennsylvania Press. Copyright © 1962 by The Trustees of the University of Pennsylvania.

J. M. B.

FOR

WILLIAM DARRID

Facile est quod facere scis

FOREWORD: DESIGN

FOR AN INQUIRY

THE WRITING OF HISTORY, for some historians at least, resembles the writing of a sonnet. Just as the sonnet form imposes on the poet a disciplined scheme of rhyme and meter, so does the historical form impose its disciplinary requirements — concerns for accuracy, honesty, clarity, relevance, and comprehensiveness in search though not in statement. Those standards and others deriving from or reinforcing them provide a meter and a rhyme for history, a disciplined scheme within which poetic license permits deliberation about the meaning and significance of the past. Truth, in that scheme, is less scientific than aesthetic. It is not on that account less grand, but it does depend in part upon the judgment and the persuasiveness of the historian. About those qualities honest men will disagree, and they will therefore disagree about statements in this inquiry.

It has a brief history of its own, a history of successive efforts to interpret the American past — as it seemed to me — to educated and intelligent men who were not historians. Like other academic historians, I have been asked by various corporations to talk to their executives about the bearing of American culture on their problems. The anxieties of business executives about the present, it has struck me on those occasions, produce accompanying confusions about the past. They do so not least because the wish to find confirmation or precedent for business preferences yields the thought that the business of America is business and always has been business. Since in fact much of the business of America has indeed been production and commerce and accumulation, it is not always easy to persuade a business audience that the United States has also larger goals and tasks, and has always had them. But businessmen have seemed to me no more parochial in their approach to history than have other groups — army and navy officers who find the true meaning of the Civil War in tactics, engineers who discover the national ethos in machinery, undergraduates who fancy that America has meant essentially an endless adventure of innocent youth. Each of those and other groups takes from a grab bag of the past plausible evidence for the excellence of its own purpose; few examine the rich range of national aspirations against the strivings, the distortions, the redemptions of the national performance. But that kind of examination, after all, is more my business than theirs.

It became my pressing business during assignments abroad where I was expected to explain the United States to Europeans whose sympathy and admiration for American promises often collided with their reasonable doubts about American behavior. They became as confused in trying to see American history as a whole as did domestic interest groups that viewed American history in separate and parochial parts. Speaking, as I had to, to both kinds of confusions, I began this inquiry into the historical meaning of the United States.

The process of inquiry, proceeding intermittently over eight years, required reassessments of familiar events, familiar propositions, familiar relationships. The resulting combinations of evidence and interpretation make up this book. It is written for those, whatever their nationality or calling, who live outside the borders of the historical profession. A synthesis of what I think I understand about the continuing performance of the American people, it is not a history of the United States but a special reading of that history. Throughout it reflects what I believe as an American, not just as an historian — what I believe as one admiring but impatient product of the culture under scrutiny.

In the United States, as elsewhere, men have made history by deciding or not deciding, by acting or not acting, by thinking and believing and molding sensibility into form. The ideas and institutions dominant in any time and place of course limited the possibilities of life in that condition, but some men have especially stretched those limits, others have expressed their culture especially well, and the culture for its part has embodied itself especially in some of those it most dignified. Such men have not necessarily been great, preeminent morally or decisive historically, but they have been at least influential or representative men. Such men seem to me to serve particularly well as nodes for the stem of written history. "The spirit of an age," said one of Andrew Jackson's eulogists, "sometimes descends to future generations in the form of a man." A nation "perpetuates what it rewards . . . the men it elevates . . . create models that are widely copied . . . for good or ill." So believed Walter Bagehot, the British political philosopher of a century ago. "The poet is a namer," Ralph Waldo Emerson once suggested, and the names the poet uses may sometimes be proper nouns. Those nouns then become no longer only the names of men but also, in T. S. Eliot's good phrase, "conceptual symbols of emotional preferences," metaphors of taste and style and purpose. I have continually and deliberately employed such metaphors as the vehicles for the interpretations in this study. Within the rhyme and meter of American history, I have made men the subject of my first concern.

Yet this study is not a venture in collective biography. Rather, I have tried to define American aspirations and to measure American achievements in terms of men who exemplified both the best and the less-than-best in the national past. The first chapter examines some of the founding fathers and some of their successors, through the time of Lincoln, in order, in a phrase of Jerome Bruner, "to condense and symbolize experience in a . . . metaphoric web." The symbol ultimately expressed in Lincoln, as I interpret it, gave unity and clarity to the noblest promise of America. The second chapter, focusing on the industrialization of the United States, attempts to suggest distortions of the national promise that grew out of too commanding an emphasis on one facet of American achievement to the partial exclusion of other pertinent and persistent hopes. The American middle class, as I see it, understood the nobility of its heritage and both the energy and the contamination that industrialists brought to it. The third chapter looks at that middle class, as it was and as it was becoming, near the turn of the twentieth century. The state of mind of the middle class, it seems to me, found metaphors in men, great and small, and found release in the policies those men pursued in this century. The fourth, fifth and sixth chapters inquire into the significance of those men and their policies in the areas, respectively, of national politics, American social life, and foreign affairs.

To the best of my ability to make it so, this inquiry is also a personal testament, a declaration of faith in the United States. It is an expression of identification, not of alienation. I am proud to be an American and glad to be identifiable with the amorphous American middle class. My pride and gladness rest in those best hopes Americans have nourished, their goals of freedom, opportunity, and shared abundance, their aspirations for an open society in which each man may know his dignity and his neighbors will respect it. But pride in those objectives makes me impatient with some aspects of the national achievement and eager to ask about the implications of American failings as well as American success.

The historian cannot be certain about what he sees when he holds the past up to a mirror of his own making. The image perforce reflects something of the beholder, and the glass, if he has raised it, refracts the light at an angle of his own choosing. This inquiry proceeds with discipline, I hope, but also with unavoidable refractions. I have selected out of the whole past those ideas and those developments that seem, in the mirror of my own commitments, best to reflect the American performance — the national promise, the changing processes for pursuing it, the changing emphases in defining it, the consequent, irregular satisfactions. I am, as it happens, an optimist. This inquiry intends to obscure no blemishes, but it does endeavor to rejoice, to describe those patterns that disclose — even for the impatient, perhaps especially for them — the nobility and the power, the mission and the magnificence of the United States.

JOHN MORTON BLUM

CONTENTS

FOREWORD: DESIGN FOR AN INQUIRY
vii

1. THE MYSTERIOUS HOPES AND FEARS
1

2. THE ENERGY OF THE NATION
29

3. A MIDDLE-CLASS COUNTRY
61

4. TO RESTORE THE ANCIENT TRUTHS
95

5. THE ULTIMATE MORALITY
123

6. THE GREATER CONCEPTION
149

ACKNOWLEDGMENTS AND SOURCES
193

INDEX
201

The
Promise of
America

☆ ☆ ☆

Chapter

1

☆ ☆ ☆ ☆ ☆

THE MYSTERIOUS
HOPES AND FEARS

THE UNITED STATES was born in history, too late to symbolize its aspirations in the exploits of an Apollo or an Arthur, too late for the "Heroick Poem" one founding father wanted. The poets found no stuff for epics, "no shadow, no antiquity, no mystery, no picturesque and gloomy wrong." In the beginning the Olympus of Americans was a place inhabited by men, not gods. The round tables of Americans were congresses of commoners who made magic only in the eloquence of informed deliberation. Yet among those commoners there were uncommon men. Their precepts and examples at once instructed and confirmed the purpose of their countrymen. Their performance shaped and sustained national beliefs, and the resulting faith polished the edges of the acts supporting it. Then uncommon men, the contours of their reputations smoothed and magnified in memory, became — or seemed — heroic.

The historical hero in America, like his counterpart in myth, symbolized ideals his career projected and his countrymen preserved. Those articles of faith, at times abused, were also perennially reaffirmed, not least by their identification with successive men of outstanding mind and temperament. In their heroes, metaphors as well as men, Americans embodied the various good hopes they merged into their best vision of the nation.

☆

Benjamin Franklin lived the first great American success story, the model, totally genuine, for latter-day heroes of fact and fiction. A poor boy, apprenticed to a printer, self-educated, self-motivated, diligent, inventive, thrifty, Franklin became the first citizen of the colonies and one of the first of the western world. A shrewd statesman and able scholar, diplomatist of American self-determination and inquirer after universal truth, he was also a *bon vivant* who often abjured the temperance he preached, and who practiced abstinence only so long as he had to. Yet this sophisticated and ingenious man, ever mindful of the needs of his audience and of the impression he intended to make, constructed in his autobiography an image of himself as plain as it was exemplary and persuasive.

The virtues Franklin praised were those on which life in the colonies depended. There was then no alternative for hard work. It alone could provide the necessities for subsistence and the surpluses for investment in future growth. Work and thrift deserved recognition, and men, as always, needed the satisfaction of esteem, at least of self-esteem, as well as the satisfactions of accomplishment. Franklin's autobiography spoke to those men and to their children, commending to them the particular good life which Franklin had earlier defined in his editorial role. "I endeavored," he recalled of his

Poor Richard's Almanac, "to make it both entertaining and useful . . . I considered it a proper vehicle for conveying instruction among the common people, who bought scarcely any other books. I therefore filled . . . the calendar with proverbial sentences . . . which contained the wisdom of many ages."

"Lost time is never found again," Poor Richard instructed. "Beware of little expenses, a small leak will sink a great ship . . . No man was e'er glorious who was not laborious . . . If you'd know the value of money, go and borrow some . . . Idleness is the greatest prodigality." "The way to wealth," Poor Richard admonished, ". . . is as plain as the way to market. It depends chiefly on two words, industry and frugality. He that gets all he can honestly, and saves all he gets . . . will certainly become rich." And therefore, Franklin implied, respected.

His own industry, visible to his neighbors, as he explained, gave him character and credit with them. Working and saving brought status as well as riches. But, Poor Richard observed, riches and status also rested upon education, for "learning, whether speculative or practical, is . . . the natural source of wealth and honor." So, too, was learning one foundation for a democratic society. The subscription libraries he had helped to establish in America, Franklin wrote, had made "the common tradesmen and farmers as intelligent as most gentlemen from other countries, and . . . contributed to the stand so generally made throughout the colonies in defense of their privileges" against English encroachments.

Although Franklin in his autobiography was of course describing his own formulae for an incomparable social ascent, he was also describing a dream which could materialize most readily in America. Only in an open society, free of the inhibiting apparatus of hereditary caste and class, could the prudential virtues so often yield riches, or could riches so surely bring status. And even in America, as Franklin understood so well, only education could keep open to deserving men the paths to wealth and honor.

Within his own lifetime Franklin became spokesman and emblem of American possibilities and of the importance of protecting them. His example heartened all men who sought to excel. The artisan, child of generations of artisans, his career fixed by centuries of local traditions, could best break through those limits by striking out on his own, by practicing — with Poor Richard — the "diligence" that "overcame difficulties," by becoming American. He could thus avail himself of the chance, the revolutionary chance, to achieve success through talent and character. That concept inhered, to be sure, in the Protestant ethic and in the experience of the colonials, but Franklin's achievement heightened the meaning of a common belief and the level of common expectations. His life, with its homely yet heroic message, dramatized American opportunity and its dependence on a free society and individual responsibility.

☆

The cluster of ideas with which Thomas Jefferson identified himself enlarged that message. Jefferson was the incomparable spokesman of human dignity, of the affinity of freedom with land, and of the relationship between freedom and nationhood. Like Franklin, versatile and cosmopolitan, at once son and sire of enlightenment, Jefferson, unlike Franklin, was inherently a political man, and in his own view of himself, a man not of the cities but of the Virginia countryside.

"Those who labor in the earth are the chosen people of God," Jefferson wrote, ". . . whose breasts He has made His peculiar deposit for substantial and genuine virtue." Corruption of morals arose, Jefferson believed, from man's dependence upon the vagaries and whims of others for whom he worked or with whom he traded. This dependence begot "subservience and venality," suffocated virtue, prepared "fit tools" for demagogues. "The proportion which the aggregate of the other classes of citizens bears in any State to that of its husbandmen, is the proportion of its unsound to its healthy parts . . . While we have land to labor then, let us never wish to see our citizens occupied at a workbench, or twirling a distaff . . . It is the manners and spirit of a people which preserve a republic in vigor."

The manners and spirit of Jefferson's Eden resembled those he knew in the Virginia Piedmont and, more intimately, in his reveries. His self-supporting yeomen, frugal and industrious perforce, were distinguished less by a quest for wealth or status than by the jealousy with which they guarded their pastoral independence and their attendant freedom in politics and mind.

Building on the base of available land, Jefferson constructed his concept of the good society through the agency of universal education, adapted to the ability of every man, directed to the "freedom and happiness" of all. "The selection of . . . youths of genius from among . . . the poor" would supply the state with talents that would otherwise "perish without use." The instruction in virtue of all, whatever their genius or station, would render "the people the safe . . . guardians of their liberties." For Jefferson, the function of education related less to potential personal success than to continuing social and political welfare. Yet education would also teach men "how to work out their greatest happiness, by showing them that it does not depend on the condition of life in which chance has placed them, but is always the result of a good conscience, good health, occupation, and freedom in all just pursuits." Jefferson's good society invited every man to live his own good life.

Jefferson's energetic politics advanced his splendid creed. Sometimes cautious, as often partisan, on occasion irascible or inconsistent, he was nevertheless at his frequent best the most convincing model of his own ideal democrat. He wrote legislation for Virginia abolishing the vestiges of primogeniture and entail, roots of aristocracy in land. The long reaches of Louisiana which he arranged to buy from France, afforded, he believed, a reserve for the safe growth of a society of husbandmen. He planned, too, a system for their education in Virginia, and hoped a similar system would evolve in the new territories, financed in part by the sale of lands which, to that end, his ordinances set aside. An avowed friend of the republicans of France, he sorrowed over the excesses of the revolution there, but while France staggered through her sea of blood, he urged patience on America. His anger rose against those of his countrymen who, inimical to France, passed laws to make criticism of their views seditious. Like the Paris mobs, but with less excuse, those Americans had rent the web of freedom, for Jefferson a seamless and inviolable whole. As his instructions for his epitaph revealed, he was proudest of his efforts to provide through education the knowledge essential for freedom, to safeguard the process vital for freedom by toleration of honest convictions, to elucidate the inalienability of freedom in the Declaration of Independence.

The truths to which that declaration gave eloquent expression were especially self-evident, Jefferson believed, to husbandmen; especially for them was republican government a realizable ideal. But all men, in his view, had an equal claim to dignity — "the mass of mankind has not been born with saddles on their backs." All men could learn to recognize the standard of reason and the restraint of virtue, all enjoyed the same natural rights. In one sense those were negative rights, rights to be free of arbitrary hierarchy and arbitrary rule. In another sense they were positive rights, rights to land and learning, to engage in commerce, to vote and hold elective office, to think and speak without constraint — freedoms in "all just pursuits." It was the task of the state to protect these rights and, where necessary, to promote them, for the state was the agent of its citizens. If it failed, they could destroy it. The freedom of man established the right of revolution.

For Jefferson, the revolution of American nationality, the War of Independence, was a symbol, writ large, of the revolution of the human spirit, its struggle for independence. In the continuing adventure of freedom, the United States had a special mission. Far from Europe and its binding past, far from its cities with their dependent merchants and more dependent mobs, far from caste and despotism, "kindly separated by nature and a wide ocean" from the corruption and conflict of the old continent, Americans could raise for the first time in history a new nation based upon the independence, dignity, and self-respect to which all men were entitled.

The idyllic freedom that Jefferson envisaged enchanted men throughout the western world. His statements complemented and enriched the soaring hopes of a revolutionary time. That enrichment, moreover, proceeded in large measure from the situation of the United States which enhanced the possibilities for reaching Jefferson's goals. No other country was so unencumbered by its customs, no other so rich in resources free men might share. Jefferson, like Franklin, prescribed under optimum conditions. But even under optimum conditions, men needed and responded to directive inspiration. It was Jefferson's heroic role to fill that need, "with instinctive perception to read the soul of the nation."

The clarity and elegance of Jefferson's prose brought beauty to the service of the principles that ruled his model for mankind. So also did his confidence and courage in the causes of free inquiry, free dissent, free men. His own proportions lent substance to his demanding faith in republican government in the United States, for him, as for his generation of Americans, "the world's best hope."

☆

To the sweep of national purpose, Alexander Hamilton added the conception of planned abundance. Hamilton left the West Indies for New York as a youth, devoid of influence, station, or wealth, but endowed with pride and grace and confidence, a devouring intelligence, and imperious ambitions. An effective pamphleteer for American independence, he became a trusted aide to General Washington. Hamilton's genius for affairs would have won him a high place in any group. As it was, by marriage and by choice he affiliated with the rich and well-born, in his view the wise and good, whose interests he considered substantially identical with those of the young nation. His literary and political contributions to the successful effort for ratification of the Constitution, along with his earlier achievements, earned him appointment as Secretary of the Treasury, an office from which he exerted an imaginative influence on the policies of the Washington Administration.

All that Hamilton planned rested on the idea — common, with variants, to Franklin and to Jefferson —of one nation whose unity of spirit and mission overwhelmed any separateness of region or group. "The people of America," Hamilton contended, "are as uniform in their interests and manners as those of any established in Europe." That unity, organized "under a vigorous government," supported by "the natural strengths and resources of the country," and "directed to a common interest, would baffle all the combinations of European jealousy to restrain our growth." The deterrence of power, Hamilton believed, provided the "best method of securing . . . peace" and independence. Since neither could be secure without domination of the Mississippi, Hamilton, like Jefferson, considered the "best interests" of the nation, the "unity of our empire," to require the annexation at the least of all land east of that river. During the crisis over Louisiana, he observed, in a phrase that distilled his lifelong view of politics, that "energy is wisdom."

Hamilton as Secretary of the Treasury had earlier associated his own ambitions with his creative program for economic growth and relied upon the energy of both to contrive the imperial destiny he cultivated for his country. The orderly simplicity of his scheme matched its systematic daring. To promote industry in the United States he borrowed from British experience, adapting it to the special needs of a continent rich in space and natural resources, poor in population, still poorer in its stock of skills, and nearly bankrupt in investment capital. First, Hamilton proposed to convert at face value the new nation's bonded debt, contracted largely during the War of Independence, and also to assume as a federal responsibility the outstanding debts of the several states. Those policies, he contended, would "justify and preserve" the confidence of "the most enlightened friends of good government," assure the "respectability of the American name," and cement the union. The new bonds issued to replace the outstanding, depreciated securities would also "furnish new resources," for they would answer, he said, "most of the purposes of money," and money was the "hinge of commerce."

A substitute for specie, the funded debt, by increasing available credit, would enable entrepreneurs to borrow on "easier and cheaper terms." The securities of the government, moreover, supplied resources for a central bank, which Hamilton designed to assist in the management of the debt and the "augmentation of the active . . . capital of the country." Wherever public banks had been chartered, he wrote, trade and industry had "been indebted to them for important aid." There lay the roots of national strength, for "the intrinsic wealth of a nation" was "to be measured, not by the abundance of . . . precious metals . . . but by the quantity of the productions of its labor and industry."

Yet adequate capital, while in itself essential, could not alone create an environment for industrialization, nor could unassisted private efforts at promotion. Entrepreneurs were inhibited by "the strong influences of habit and . . . imitation; fear of want of success in untried enterprises; the intrinsic difficulties incident to . . . competition." Consequently there arose the need, indeed the obligation, for public initiative. Accordingly Hamilton advocated favorable laws of incorporation, inducements to the immigration of skilled labor, inspection of the quality of manufactured goods, federal construction of roads and waterways, and especially a protective tariff. In selecting industries for protection, he favored those subservient to national defense, and those complementary to natural resources, susceptible to mechanization, and central to the process of further growth. The encouragement of manufactures, he believed, would create demands for the goods and services of an expanding agriculture and commerce, whose prosperity in turn would enlarge the markets for industrial products, while the resulting surpluses of every sector spurred new investment.

"Everything tending to establish substantial and permanent order in the affairs of a country, to increase the total mass of industry and opulence," Hamilton concluded, "is ultimately beneficial to every part of it." Private interests and local interests were for him at one with national interests. The energy of his system penetrated and advanced them all. He was the entrepreneur of the promotive state with its prospectus for national power, for national wealth, and for individual gain, particularly for the rich — the investors and managers, but also, in lesser degree, for wage-earners and farmers. Freedom concerned him less than did structure and administration. His vision, neither frugal, rural, nor egalitarian, was bullish, materialistic, aristocratic. It was always also patriotic, focused upon the objective he early defined as "noble and magnificent," "the perspective of a great Federal Republic, closely linked in the pursuit of a common interest, tranquil and prosperous at home, respectable abroad." He gave an adventurous, heroic cadence to the language of industry and finance. He symbolized their capacity, with federal assistance, for building a mighty economy, the basis for world power, the cornucopia of unprecedented comfort.

☆

Franklin, Jefferson, and Hamilton, all three exultantly American, considered the nation the receptacle of their purpose and the vehicle for its ultimate satisfaction. They had drawn the sets of values they exemplified from their culture, which for its part reabsorbed their faith and embodied it in the idea of the United States. The mirror of that idea reflected George Washington, for all Americans, wrote Parson Weems, "the Patriot Hero of our Revolution, the Christian Statesman of our Republic, great in goodness, good in greatness." The hard fiber of Washington supported the soft sentimentality of Weems. Washington excelled as planter, woodsman, soldier, governor. He brought stature to the demands and fortitude to the struggles for independence. Born to ordinary circumstances, he achieved patrician status and gave respectability to wealth.

Even before his death, the life of Washington had merged with the history of his country, the legend of Washington with its incipient legend. Washington's aloofness, Washington's majesty qualified him, "a Roman hero and a Grecian god," to serve as an abstraction that contained the separate, unsynthesized aspirations of his countrymen. So, too, the facts of his career evoked sentiments which the newly independent nation harnessed for its own survival, sentiments associated with character and duty, sacrifice and loyalty — in the words of Washington's most popular biographer, "piety and patriotism . . . industry and honor . . . SELF ESTEEM and UNIVERSAL RESPECT."

Like Franklin in his autobiography, moreover, Washington in his "Farewell Address" suggested a metaphor of himself which he intended to prevail. "The union of government which constitutes you one people," he there told his fellow-citizens, ". . . is a main pillar . . . of your real independence, the support of your tranquillity at home, your peace abroad, of your safety, of your prosperity, of that very liberty which you so highly prize." "That your Union . . . may be perpetual," he warned against the divisiveness of sectional attachments, the "baneful effects of the spirit of party," the potentialities for mischief in foreign alliances and intrigues. "The name of AMERICAN," he said, "which belongs to you, in your national capacity, must always exalt the just pride of patriotism more than any appellation derived from local discriminations." The name of American patriotism was Washington, a symbol of reverence, for a century and more "a primary . . . an ultimate relation, like the Pole Star."

☆

Social mobility, the prudential virtues, and universal education; land, free government, free thought, and human dignity; economic plenty and industrial power — all these sometimes contradictory elements were reconciled within one overarching edifice, that of the American nation, the United States. The various parts merged to form the promise of American life. It was a promise that offered the chance of fulfillment to men of diverse ambitions and diverse ideals. It was, furthermore, a promise which experience frequently confirmed. Consequently it was a revolutionary promise, exciting new expectations in men everywhere, equating those expectations with the successful American revolution, an adventure in national independence and self-consciousness as well as in democratic society and self-government.

In Europe the revolutionary impact of the American message was both personal and national. It was a personal revolution for a man to leave the village of his ancestors, traverse the ocean, and settle in a strange new land. The absence of opportunity pushed emigrants from their homes. The presence of opportunity drew them to the United States. The seeming nearness of comfort and social advantage were perhaps the prime attractions, but other lines of the magnetic field also exerted a transatlantic pull. In that way the United States acquired most of its people, the labor it needed, the progenitors of talents indispensable for a demanding future. Those who responded to the attractions of America were prepared, moreover, if not at once then by rapid stages, to absorb the total implications of its heroic imagery.

So also did the nation acquire much of its capital from the migration of money. As the vistas of Hamilton's imagination opened in reality, the savings of Europe, especially of Great Britain, pursued profits in the United States, supplying some of the funds that transformed a backward area into an industrial colossus. That metamorphosis, a revolution in itself, added the allure of attainment to the predictions of the image.

American success also whetted the yearnings of the aspiring nationalities of the world. Like Americans themselves, they associated with American independence and nationhood the characteristics of freedom and of abundance. The self-determination of peoples came to connote both democracy and material progress, a combination that commanded the revolutionary fervor of nationalists in Europe and Latin America. In Mexico, Argentina, and Colombia, in Italy, Poland, Greece,

Hungary and Germany, movements for national independence and national confederation drew inspiration from the example of the United States. That inspiration was cultivated by American sympathies that heartened, though they did not actually aid, the revolutionists of Europe. Indeed the Monroe Doctrine, while disavowing American involvement "in the wars of European powers, in matters relating to themselves," and in "their internal concerns," nevertheless asserted "sentiments . . . most friendly, in favor of the liberty and happiness" of European peoples.

More particularly, the rhetoric of that doctrine allied the United States with the quest for freedom and independence in the whole of the Americas. As a matter of "principle in which the rights and interests of the United States" were involved, the western continents were "henceforth not to be considered as subjects for future colonization by any European Power." Any attempt by those powers, moreover, to extend their political system "to any portion of this Hemisphere," was declared "dangerous" to the peace and safety and happiness of the United States.

This statement of policy expressed the dominant national conviction, so redolent of Jefferson and Washington, that the two worlds of Europe and America were separated as much by the potentialities of their cultures as by the span of the ocean. The old was the depraved. The new was the virtuous, inviting men to share its spiritual and material bounty. The United States, model of the new, broadcast its commitment to its mission, its appointed duty to speed the inexorable triumph of the good.

The very success of the national experience fed national confidence, and confidence, as so often in the affairs of men, occasioned some arrogance about the privileges of power. So it was that a host of Americans concluded that they had not only an exemplary but also a militant function. They viewed themselves as a people chosen to use force, if necessary, "to overspread and possess the whole of the continent which Providence has given us for the development of the great experiment of liberty and federated self-government." It was the presumed destiny of the United States to arrogate to itself the lands of Indians, Mexicans and Spaniards, and to bring to those lands American concepts of freedom and American uses of property. So a sometimes facile conscience eased the path of conquest, and the promise of America, in most ways benign, put on at times a predatory mask. And yet beneath the mask the rapacious spirit yielded, after conquest, to the principles of freedom and abundance, for no territory taken by arms or treaty was long excluded from full participation in the nation. Indeed westering Americans carried with them the symbols of Franklin, Jefferson, and Hamilton, and as the nation moved, the shadows of its culture lengthened, but their pattern remained essentially unchanged.

☆

The American ethos and its implications affected most profoundly the people of the United States. During the half-century after 1800 the ideals of freedom, dignity, mobility, and plenty infused the proliferating movements for domestic reform. The nation made continual, impressive progress toward a wider franchise, women's rights, free public education, free land — toward a more open society, a larger scope for talent. It progressed, too, not only toward industrialism but also toward a broader distribution of the wealth that industrialism produced. These developments could have occurred so quickly only in a country as lavishly endowed as was the United States, but the sense of purpose that Americans held determined in part the development of their endowment. Their expectations, so often stated, so often satisfied, seemed more and more to be the driveshaft in the national effort.

Correspondingly, latter-day American heroes were identified with values characteristic of their predecessors, but now the metaphors were cruder, for the ebullient nineteenth century sometimes demanded bumptious qualities of candidates for its acropolis. One such was Andrew Jackson. Jeffersonian precepts saturated his rhetoric and his belief in government "void of pomp, protecting all and granting favors to none, dispensing its blessings, like the dews of Heaven, unseen and unfelt save in the freshness and beauty they contribute to produce." Jackson also met the prescriptions of Franklin. "Born a simple citizen," his eulogist related, ". . . he became great by no other means than the energy of his own character . . . Severe discipline and poverty, inured him, in early life, to great hardship and industry, and . . . he seems to have been an orphan from the plough to the presidency."

Farmers and workingmen could readily admire Jackson and his program, especially his confidence in their capacity to hold public office and his concern for their chances to earn success in any chosen calling. So, too, could the commercial middle class rejoice in Jacksonian democracy. Its hero and his associates were the champions of public policies that opened opportunities in trade and finance to entrepreneurs previously excluded by restrictive laws or charters. By Jackson's time, the energy of private promotion had so quickened that the economy could develop in a laissez-faire environment. While abandoning most of Hamilton's techniques and attacking many of the privileges they had nourished, the Jacksonians supported his ultimate object of national strength, founded in expanding national wealth and its compatibility with private gain. Hamilton's elitism had been subordinated to the contradictory demands of the rising democratic faith and cult of success. The resultant synthesis, unabashedly bourgeois, was no less vital on that account, particularly among a people who were virtually all self-consciously of, or aspiring to, the middle class. And patriotism, a sentiment rarely foreign to middle class men, was represented magnificently in Jackson, a victorious soldier and ardent unionist.

Indeed Jackson, "Old Hickory," the conqueror of the British and the Spanish, the Indian fighter, the prickly defender of personal honor, exuded a spirit which the more prudential of his countrymen may have honored partly because it replaced something which they, in their day-to-day lives, had lost. Yet Jackson, a wealthy planter and accomplished politician, was by no means atavistic. Davy Crockett claimed that quality for himself. "Fresh from the backwoods, half horse, half alligator," he could "wade the Mississippi, leap the Ohio, ride like a streak of lightning," and whip his weight in wildcats. Crockett reflected the nation's lingering, pastoral bias clothed in buckskin. His was a wild freedom and a synthetic success that took him from Tennessee to Congress, then to the banquet circuit, and eventually to the Whig Party. It used him disingenuously, as it did the log cabin and hard cider, as a front for its anti-Jacksonian program. But Crockett's brave death at the Alamo, defending manifest destiny, returned him to the fold for which he had been invented.

The myth of Crockett was too comic, the symbol of Jackson

too tinged by the fiery partisanship of his politics, to permit either, or both together, to reconcile the various constitutents of the national culture. Americans had recognizable ideals, ideals long held and long developed, ideals identified with heroic men and their achievements, ideals combined in nationhood, but Americans had no ideology. They had, rather, an unsystematic sense of the workable unity of sundry values, an image of themselves and their aspirations which had yet to be expressed, even unsystematically, in its whole range. That image, if it was to endure, needed a poet of its own to infuse it with poignancy and ambiguity — poignancy in order to extend its sway over men's emotions, ambiguity in order to cast its spell over those otherwise resistant.

☆

There were many who wrote hymns to the image of America, but its poet laureate, even when he scolded, was Ralph Waldo Emerson. Emerson sang of liberation and fulfillment, of the equal share of every man in divine inspiration and thus in human dignity. Each man could reach his glory if only he pursued it freely and courageously, and each so doing, each flowering in his private plot, made rich and verdant the wonderful garden of the whole community. The capacity of man derived from his rapport with Nature, Nature's God, and God-inspired systems and designs for revealing the paths to true satisfaction. Of these designs, one was the state whose function was to liberate the moral influence of its every citizen. That moral influence Emerson called character, by which he meant a native genius for recognizing the special faculty that enabled each man "to do easily some feat impossible to any other." The true equality of men was spiritual; the true liberty of men was to find themselves; the true democracy left finding unimpeded. Thus a godly nation encouraged godly lives. Thus the image of America, if it were godly, became religious.

So also did its separate ingredients. Most obviously, Emerson preserved the Eden of Jefferson while he spiritualized it. The freedoms Jefferson pronounced were Emerson's freedoms. The satisfactions and the safety Jefferson found in land, Emerson found in nature, which he capitalized by way of sanctification. Nature, in this context, never wore a "mean expression." Ethical to the "bone and marrow," it was the university of powerful minds, its beauties reforming in them. The natural man best understood and used his natural rights.

Emerson preserved as much of Franklin, turning Poor Richard's earthly strictures into sweeter sentiments, giving them a spiritual twist without costing them their practicality. "A man is fed," Emerson wrote, "not that he may be fed, but that he may work." Industry, for him, still brought success, but essentially the success of contentment. "Discontent," in contrast, was the "want of self-reliance," an "infirmity of will." True status came from the integrity of self-expression. "Do your work," Emerson taught, "respecting the excellence of the work, and not its acceptableness . . . Profligacy consists not in spending years of time or chests of money — but in spending them off the line of your career . . . Spend after your genius." But, he suggested, take care not to spend too much: "Want is the growing giant whom the coat of Have was never large enough to cover."

If Franklin's maxims now stretched beyond the marketplace, they were no less valid there. Commerce, for Emerson, was a game of skill, "which every man cannot play," but there was always reason "in the man," he wrote, "for his good . . . fortune, and so in making money." For those whom nature appropriately endowed, business was a religious calling — an idea not new with Emerson, but bred in him. "The coin," he proposed, "is a delicate meter of civil, social and moral changes." By their success, then, he would know the chosen merchants, and in their success, the entire nation could profit, provided that they had the proper spirit. That spirit had produced the machines, the division of labor, the material benefits that could, if the wealthy were wise stewards, "give all access to the masterpieces of art and nature."

Something, then, of Hamilton was also preserved. Emerson, moreover, was no leveler. On the contrary, spiritual equality called upon the business instinct to organize and produce and thereby to thrive. And by Emerson's time, the minimized state, which he exalted, encouraged the ventures Hamilton had endorsed. Hamilton, as much as Franklin, would doubtless have applauded the commercial metaphor that Emerson occasionally adopted. Only a poet basically at home in a business civilization could have written, as he did, that "counting-room maxims liberally expounded are laws of the universe," that "the merchant's economy is a coarse symbol of the soul's economy."

Yet Emerson, consummate transcendentalist, transcended his business civilization. As he put it in his continuing metaphor, man's "true thrift is always to spend on the higher plane; to invest and invest, with keener avarice, that he may spend in spiritual creation and not in augmenting animal existence." Fulfillment, in the end, was not material; success, not worldly; liberty, not commercial. Man was God's moral creature, and though the spirit could properly reveal itself in many ways, the matter of first importance was the integrity and the freedom of the process of self-expression. So, too, with the nation, whose true strength lay not in wealth or might, but in its glowing soul. Emerson's open society was above all a moral society, indeed a religious society, fashioned in the image he attributed to God.

☆

The image Emerson attributed to America reached for that summit but fell short especially on one account — there was no success or plenty, no dignity or freedom for the Negro. So long as slavery existed, the American image, however plausible, was pretentious. The poet of the image was of course an Abolitionist, and as he understood, the image had to have a confirming statesman, too. "Every heroic act," he wrote, ". . . causes the place and the bystanders to shine." Nations therefore needed heroes, whose sure instincts, Emerson believed with an Hegelian certitude, would serve their best, their root ideals. He rejoiced when Lincoln put things right.

Abraham Lincoln, for Emerson, personified the image of America. Lincoln, he eulogized, was "a plain man of the people . . . a man without vices . . . a great worker . . . sound to the core, cheerful, persistent . . . tolerant and accessible to all; fair-minded . . . affable . . . noble . . . His occupying the chair of state was a triumph of the good sense of mankind, and of the public conscience. This middle-class country had got a middle-class president, at last. Yes, in manners and sympathies, but not in powers, for his powers were superior."

That was the nub of it. Lincoln's virtues were American but also immanently heroic virtues. Lincoln was everybody's

American, in time even in the South, the boy's, the farmer's,
the laborer's, the businessman's, the soldier's. They all saw
themselves in him. A man of the soil, self-made, self-taught, a
successful man in every meaning of success, withal a man of
humor and patience and compassion, Lincoln was the arche-
typical American hero, the ultimate good man. "I am a living
witness," the President told Ohio troops, "that any one of
your children may look to come here as my father's child
has . . . that each of you may have, through this free government · . . an open field and a fair chance for your industry,
enterprise, and intelligence."

With Franklin's wit and naturalness, he followed Franklin's precepts as far as Franklin had, no further. With Hamilton's political and administrative energy, but also with humility, he promoted the agencies for wealth and strength that
Hamilton had favored. With Jefferson's hope and Emerson's
soulfulness, he advanced their freedoms and ideals. Most emphatically, with his certain knowledge of priority, he put the
whole power of those values and of his enveloping person in
the service of the legacy of Washington, the service of perpetual union. When the awful struggle of his tenure ended in his
martyrdom, it had to be Lincoln — not history, not politics,
not even war — it had to be Lincoln who freed the slaves and
saved the union. He died, it seemed, for what he lived; he
exemplified what he preserved.

The myths after Lincoln, founded securely on his real
achievements, made him the embodiment of the American
ethos and embodied that ethos in him. In fact, as much as in
symbol, he performed with an awareness of heritage and destiny, and thus of terrible responsibility. The issue of the Civil
War, he wrote when it began, embraced "more than the fate

of the United States." It tested the future of "free government upon the earth." The war was the very hinge of fate. Yet when it ended, Lincoln, without malice even in the extremes of distress, asked for the binding up of the wounds of battle, for charity from all for all. He asked then, as he always had, not for God — for right and justice — to join his side, but for himself to know and choose the side of God. He knew, as intuitively he had always known, that even the highest aspirations, indeed especially these, worked to their triumph in the affairs of men only in the company of constant duty and recurrent tragedy.

The sadness of Lincoln and the years his spirit dominated marked the coming of age of the national ethos. From Lincoln, from their experience with him, Americans learned, though they might sometimes forget, that no ideal was free from corruption, no people free of evil, no destiny immune from disaster. Yet the severity of the trial and the gravity of the verdict deepened the convictions at stake. The second war of American nationality drove forward the implications of the first.

That was the message that informed the postwar primers of American children, the Fourth of July orations their parents heard, the editorial rooms of every Emporia, the evenings at every Chautauqua. The expectation of general plenty, personal success, individual freedom, constituted a unified faith at home, confirmed in blood, identified with pride in nation, consumed or exported in a single package. What Americans learned to believe about Lincoln, they were conditioned, in their noble moments, to demand of themselves. "Lincoln was great because he was good," the textbooks said; Lincoln was human dignity and morality and fulfillment. The heroic symbols of a receding past were merged in his inclusive passion. He summed them up; he redeemed them all.

Consequently, for his countrymen Lincoln was, more than anyone else had ever been or has yet become, "thoroughly American," in Emerson's words, an "heroic figure in the center of an heroic epoch . . . the true history of the American people in his time." As Emerson also said, he evoked among men everywhere "the mysterious hopes and fears . . . connected with the name and institutions of America." He was the best vision of the nation.

Chapter

2

★ ☆ ☆ ☆ ☆

THE ENERGY

OF THE NATION

IN THE DECADES after Appomattox, the metaphors of American culture served, as actuality could not, to reconcile divergent national aspirations. For the spiritual children of Emerson, Lincoln was the symbol of the redemption and the fulfillment of the whole moral purpose of America. With victory in the Civil War, as they interpreted it, freedom and opportunity and the dignity of man would be ensured at last by and within the federal union. The good and the nation would be one. The war, however, was not long over before they began to fear that they had lost their cause. From their point of view, there was abroad in the land something crass and fetid and alien. "We hoped," Emerson wrote, "that in the peace . . . a great expansion would follow in the mind of the country; grand views in every direction . . . But the energy of the nation seems to have expended itself in the war."

The nation, however, was not without energy. On the contrary, what distressed Emerson derived largely from the power of advancing industrialism with all its implications. And industrialism was by no means alien. Rather, from the time of

independence Americans had given a high priority to economic development, whether through the modified mercantil-
ism of Hamilton or the tempered laissez-faire of the Jacksonians. In one way and another, public policy had continuously
encouraged industrialization as the means to transform the
bounty of nature into the strengths and comforts of an abundant society. So, too, had capitalism in its various forms been
the preferred national system for the organization of industrialism.

Its steady growth hastened during the war and accelerating
thereafter, industrialism rapidly reached its assigned goals.
Never before had any people experienced a multiplication of
facilities comparable to that in the United States during the
forty years after Lincoln's election. In that period, the railroad
network, already well established east of the Mississippi,
spread to the Pacific. Thirty thousand railway miles became
almost two hundred and sixty thousand. The growth of intra-
urban lines was equally dramatic, and as the telegraph followed the rails, so did the telephone get a sure start toward
overhauling its more clumsy predecessor. In 1860 the United
States was producing modest quantities of steel and petro-
leum. By 1900 the nation led all others in the manufacture of
steel, and the oil industry, its main product still kerosene, had
gained a central importance in the economy. Electricity, unknown in 1860 for industrial purposes, was enjoying a rich
dawn. Manufactured textiles and dressed meats had almost
replaced home production of those commodities.

A self-congratulatory wonder at the sheer magnitude of
those and similar accomplishments appeased but could not
still the conscience of Americans who were jealous of their
heritage. While industry achieved the production of plenty,

its structure, and the structure it imparted to society, threatened the satisfaction of persisting aspirations for individual success and freedom. While capitalism adapted to the demands of a massive market, its institutions acquired privileges and immunities which earlier generations had designed for the benefit of the common man. Americans for the most part welcomed industrialism, but they worried about the pattern of its organization and the distribution of its fruits.

☆

Before the Civil War, the pattern characteristic of American industry had begun to appear in textiles and railroading. In the years after the war, that pattern, with significant variations that never obscured it, stamped railroading, oil and steel, and eventually electricals, chemicals, and other basic industries. The pattern did not create itself. Rather, American managers shaped enterprise to take advantage of the domestic market, the largest free market of the nineteenth century. As improvements in transportation opened a continental area to population and commerce, as improvements in communications carried to that area a common culture and its tastes, manufacturers designed methods of production and distribution suitable to their opportunities for sales and profits. In the inviting American market, swollen by continuous immigration, the prospect of large sales continually excited new expectations of profit. The premium which the nature of the market placed upon standardized mass production, as well as the inherent desirability of minimizing costs, led industrialists to work toward continuous processes of manufacture facilitated by maximum mechanization. The desirability of mechanization arose, too, from periodic paucity of a competent labor supply for one industry or another at various stages of its growth.

Those conditions, conducive to technical and managerial innovation, fostered rapid obsolescence of plant and equipment. Both the conditions and the obsolescence, moreover, encouraged entrepreneurs, if they were to succeed, to start with a large investment and to maintain a large liquid reserve. Generous working capital also permitted the purchase of raw materials in a quantity whose very abundance heightened the preference of producers for large sales at not much more than marginal prices. This entire situation commended to discerning businessmen the pattern for American industry — capitalistic from the beginning; blessed with a sufficient domestic market and a sufficient domestic supply; expansive and technological, consequently both adaptive and vulnerable to change; and on these and related accounts, tending typically to large size.

The tendency to bigness, perhaps the most marked quality of American capitalism, generated some of its own momentum. Once an enterprise had accumulated ample funds and knowledgeable personnel, it could exploit the possibilities of vertical integration. There were, of course, potential savings in acquiring ownership of sources of primary and secondary supplies and services. Vertical organization also permitted, though it did not necessarily insure, the reduction of managerial overhead and the efficiencies of controlled rates and dimensions in the flow of materials from extraction through transportation, assembly, manufacture and distribution. So, too, the interrelationship among advancing technologies and the logic of joint costs encouraged diversification, especially for those many firms concerned with applications of science and engineering to business, and with bigness in buying, managing, and selling. The conditions of the economy stimulated the entrepreneur to seize the advantages of size; the economy of size in turn led him further in the same direction.

Prospects for profit, particularly for profit in big organizations engaged in growing industries, occasioned the spurts of investment that periodically built productive capacity beyond immediate national needs. This sporadic over-feeding supplied some of the means for its own ultimate satisfaction. Throughout the nineteenth century it also, in the absence of any theory or medium of general control, quickened the rate and intensified the severity of the business cycle. Even in boom times, moreover, it created instability within those industries which suffered for the while from surplus capacity. The inability of managers and investors to moderate the business cycle gave them an extra sense of urgency about eliminating the perils of undisciplined competition for lagging sales. And to that end, they made bigness even bigger.

When capacity exceeded demand, as at times it did in many industries, competing firms ordinarily resorted, if they could, to arrangements that divided trade and limited production in order to guarantee prices and profits adequate for survival. Heavy industries were particularly vulnerable to the debilitations of competition, and therefore particularly avid to overcome them. The railroads, first of the American big businesses, suffered, as in lesser degree did their successors, from the pressure of huge indebtedness. Whether or not trains ran, whether with full or partial loads, the interest on outstanding bonds had to be paid if owners were to escape bankruptcy, if managers were to hold their jobs, and if lenders were to remain content and ready to invest again. Also fixed in season and out were the large costs of managerial salaries and of speedy obsolescence. Any regular, unit price that protected solvency had to cover not only those and other constant costs but also the variable costs of labor, raw material, and depreciation — variable costs involved in moving a unit of freight over a mile of track, or in producing an ingot of steel or a barrel of oil. But when capacity temporarily exceeded demand and competitors cut prices, each seeking to enlarge his share of trade, the resulting struggle pushed unit prices down. Anything that remained after variable costs were met was preferable to nothing at all for allocation toward the inescapable obligations of debt and obsolescence. Yet price cutting and retaliation could terminate in disaster. Even the stronger firms staggered; as for the weaker firms, the first into bankruptcy, they could then by virtue of their failure insulate or reduce their bonded debt and then compete at some advantage over their now threatened rivals.

This recurrent situation fastened a mood of insecurity on the business community, on its titans not least. One remarked "the fear that exists among capitalists." Andrew Carnegie confessed himself "overwhelmed by business cares." John D. Rockefeller recalled the unending anxiety of "work by day and worry by night." Typically "scary," American business managers and financiers yearned for certainty and stability. The state of nature of heavy industry resembled that which Thomas Hobbes had imagined, its citizens timorous men in search of the protection of leviathans.

The social contract the industrialists adopted was that most obviously at hand, the combination of competing units. Voluntary cooperation through pools and trade agreements moderated competition, but experience with them revealed their unsuitability to adequate discipline and administration. Mergers and voting trusts of various kinds permitted, as cooperation did not, the planning and penetration of policy, the imposition by unified management of conditions desirable for stability. Of all the devices for consolidation, the holding company had been developed into the most effective by the turn of the century. The holding company, a corporation authorized to own stock in other corporations, had the legal advantages of corporate status. It could be built in tiers that enabled it to control many subsidiaries through only a fractional ownership, and thus to use its financial resources with scope and flexibility. It could consolidate within one system both horizontal and vertical combinations. During the 1890's such consolidations came to dominate every basic industry, though very few were without rivals. Those consolidations, moreover, were reaching proportions which seemed gigantic. Indeed one of them, the United States Steel Corporation, a consolidation of consolidations effected in 1901, for the first time stretched bigness beyond one billion dollars, the stated value of its securities.

The consolidation of business was in its own way an achievement as impressive as the productivity of industry. Consolidation provided managers with the means to protect themselves and their investors, and if they chose, their employees and customers, too, from the vicissitudes of unregulated competition. The waste and uncertainty of competition were among the factors that held wages down and made employment irregular. The losses sustained in price wars forced damaged firms to try to balance their accounts by overcharging customers who had no alternative supplier. With consolidation, manufacturers, while securing their own profits, could offer their customers steady prices. Those customers could then manage their businesses more systematically and ordinarily therefore more profitably. Though the ultimate consumer had usually to pay the charges accumulated by administered pricing, the regularities and the risklessness of consolidation appealed to most established businessmen. "The greatest prosperity," one consolidator put it, "will come from the most perfect stability."

Consolidation, furthermore, helped decent men to discipline the rogues of whom business had always had an ample quota. The chaos of unchecked competition in industry and finance left the innocent at the mercy of the unscrupulous, the speculators who never hesitated, in their calculating greed, to destroy a business or smash a market. In contrast, most financiers who promoted the great consolidations and appointed their managers realized that their private gain depended upon expanding businesses and stabilizing markets. Ethical business behavior, so important for those objectives, was most probable in an environment of "sweet order." Consolidation therefore appeared to be an instrument of morality as well as of profit. Thomas A. Edison called his foremost rival in the market for electric motors a man "gone crazy." J. Pierpont Morgan, the Jupiter of American finance, used the verb "demoralize" as a synonym for "compete." He and his associates, Morgan believed, were the statesmen of industrial order, philosopher kings capable of managing their realms without outside supervision or interference.

That was the universal conviction of the consolidators. They took pride in the productivity of the mighty systems they governed. They took pride in the strength they bestowed on the nation. They took pride, above all, in their own "safe

hands." Their faith swelled by the evidence of their achievements, they were sure that they were the deserving, responsible, Christian men "to whom God in his infinite wisdom has
given control of the property interests of the country."

☆

The consolidators' legitimate satisfaction in their success
gave them absolute confidence in their own virtue. Though
the essence of their success was material, though it derived in
large part from the economic situation they perceived, their
ethic gave it a spiritual gloss. The wealthy viewed themselves,
as in the past they often had, as a natural elite. American culture had long tended to allow that commerce was one mirror
of the universe. To the support of that presumption, the masters of industry now summoned the imposing vocabulary of
Darwinian biology. When commerce and the universe were
both held to follow the laws of natural selection, it was easy
for the rich to conclude that they were the finest tigers in the
jungle. This kind of Social Darwinism provided a glamorous
metaphor for modernizing old assumptions. The mechanical
laws of competition of Adam Smith now became the dynamic
laws of Herbert Spencer and his American disciples. Belief in
the manifestation of grace in wealth was now assimilated into
belief in the survival of the fittest, with its corollary dictum
that the laws of evolution, decreed by God, assured the triumph of the best. Circular though the argument was, its powerful reassertions in the names of science and of truth enhanced its plausibility.

The folklore of the new elitism twisted the precepts of older
formulae for success. The captains of industry and finance
liked to consider their origins humble, though few began their

march to eminence without singular advantages. They liked to interpret their struggle to power as the ordeal of an individual, though none competed except in association with institutions that depended on many men. They liked to attribute their ascent to work and thrift, though many of them, while assiduous, were also often speculators, and all of them were the organizers and the beneficiaries of the risks of thousands of investors. They also liked to think that their imperial insights derived from God, though all of their imperial decisions were secular. Their faith respected none of these anomalies. As one observer summarized their creed: "Irreligion, dissoluteness, and pessimism — supposed naturally to go together — could never prosper; they were incompatible with efficiency. That was the supreme test."

One supreme symbol of the whole creed was Andrew Carnegie. Born in Scotland in the impoverished family of a hand-loom weaver, Carnegie emigrated to the United States while still a boy. His zeal for practical learning, hard work and influential friends made him within a dozen years a division superintendent on the Pennsylvania Railroad. Astuteness in investment soon brought him to iron and then to steel. Always a joyous salesman of his products, himself not the least, Carnegie was also a shrewd judge of talent. With his associates and subordinates in finance, engineering and management, he took adroit advangage of the opportunities available in the market, the technology and the organization of American industry. By 1890 his companies constituted the largest and richest system in the steel business.

As an industrial strategist, Carnegie set a style that the preeminent enterprisers of his time endorsed. He had begun as the poorest of those who became magnificently rich, and some of the more privileged, envying the heroic scale of his success, invented synthetic childhood hardships for themselves. He wrote more than did any of his peers about industrial struggle and survival, always in the language of Charles Darwin and Herbert Spencer, and always with the stark assumption that competition, even in steel, remained open, effective, even glorious. Like the other Olympians of wealth, he was dedicated to the prudential ethic and its vigorous practice, a "firm believer," as he put it, "in the doctrine that people deserving necessary assistance . . . usually receive it." In expressing that faith, Carnegie was much gentler than most of the very rich, men like Thomas Mellon, sire of a great financial dynasty. As a young man, Mellon by his own account was delighted with Franklin's autobiography and its "wider view of life." "Earnest, cautious and painstaking," he husbanded his means, chose a wife for her station and dowry, "never neglected" his "private affairs." Naturally he advised his sons against the "folly of soldiering" during the Civil War. "Poverty," Mellon reflected, "may be a misfortune to the weaklings who are without courage or ability to overcome it, but it is a blessing to young men of ordinary force of character."

Carnegie, in contrast, would not settle for prudence and money alone as the means and end of a good life. The impulse that drove him to seek wealth and power, the compulsion that led him to concentrate on steel, "putting all his eggs in one basket and then watching the basket," the hunger he appeased by purchasing castles in Scotland — all these warred with his wish to do good. He worried about the degradation of thinking "wholly upon the way to make more money," and he contemplated alternative satisfactions, personal and altruistic, in an Oxford education, a London town house, "control-

ling interest in some newspaper or live review . . . taking
part in public matters, especially those connected with education and improvement of the poorer classes." The systematic
giving of Carnegie's late years, his endowments of libraries,
scholarship, and the quest for permanent world peace, benefited the indigent, the intellectual, and the idealistic. More
important, his munificence established for others like him, including the younger Mellons, the Rockefellers, Guggenheims,
and Fords, the "duty of the man of wealth" to "consider all
surplus revenues . . . as trust funds . . . to administer in
the manner . . . best calculated to provide the most beneficial results for the community." A stewardship of wealth on
the imperial scale that Carnegie defined had a genuine nobility.

So, to a degree, had the man himself — a living proof, however extraordinary, of the continuing opportunities of Americans, a self-conscious champion, in his writings at least, of the
dignity and freedom of man, a strong agent for the manufacture and distribution of abundance. But to a degree also his
appearance was specious. Though Carnegie cultivated a reputation for identification with the poor, he did not expend his
enormous wealth in raising the near-subsistence wages of the
laborers in his employ. Rather, he sought seclusion while his
associates, with his approval, broke strikes with violence. The
competition he really enjoyed was governed by his own rules
for his own advantages, and his castles made queer homes for
his alleged humility. Even in stewardship he was responsible
in the end only to his own whims, however laudable, and
never to the whole community whose efforts, he admitted,
had contributed to his fortune.

No one man fully typified the performance and the creed of

the consolidators, no one man fully symbolized them in the public mind, but Carnegie fared better than the others. In his day, compared to him, John D. Rockefeller seemed more predatory, partly because his manner was pinched and remote, partly because the rough methods of his oil companies were subject, as Carnegie's were not, to continual exposure in the courts and press. The railroad barons won evil reputations as much because of their ingenuous disdain for their customers as because of the vigor and, at times, extravagance of their detractors. J. P. Morgan suffered from his identification with Wall Street, ever a folk symbol of secret and malign power. Yet many Americans frankly admired great wealth and all who acquired it. Some of the more audacious or fanciful of those admirers saw in the consolidators, in their methods and their way of life, models for personal emulation; others, more passive, read softened stories of the very rich with the wonder of contented children. For the admiring, the aspiring, the wonderful, Andrew Carnegie provided an heroic figure, for he was ambiguous enough, by his own intent, at once to represent much of the manner and achievement of the consolidators and much of the spirit of their times. Still, not even Carnegie, much less his fellows, could escape the distrust and bitterness that the techniques of industrial management sometimes engendered.

☆

The observable facts of the industrial situation argued against the full acceptance of the consolidator's creed with all its scaffolding, especially within a culture for which wealth had always been only one of a complex of hopes. It was obvious, as in the case of Carnegie and steel, that in the face of competition, the timorous tigers of the business jungle preferred the safety of consolidation to the dangers of a contest of prowess. Though their partisans stretched the analogy of evolution to bless the victorious institutions, corporations seemed strange receptacles for either Providence or science to have chosen for unfolding its designs. More important, consolidation, indeed bigness itself, however useful, altered the nature of opportunity available to Americans. As industries grew and institutionalized, it took more and more capital to launch an enterprise. The command over capital that existing enterprises enjoyed, and the power they had to crush a newcomer, multiplied the problems and the risks of expectant entrepreneurs. The outlets for ambition came increasingly to lie within the bureaucracies of bigness which needed continually more clerical, technical, professional and executive personnel. Some of those so employed felt they had less choice, less range and pace of rise, than the middle class of earlier generations.

In absolute terms, there was more room in the middle than ever before for the ambitious poor. Still, a growing proportion of those born to poverty met constraints in seeking access to the professions and to the industrial bureaucracy. The education of the poor, as the century wore on, prepared them more and more for routine work, or for careers as tradesmen and small proprietors, callings especially exposed to the hazards of the business cycle and the power of large corporations.

Indeed industrialists did not ordinarily treat education as a vehicle for mobility. They concentrated instead on persuading schools to teach mechanical skills, useful in production and for employment, but weak levers for self-promotion to middle class gentility. So, too, the wealthy made engineering education one favorite recipient of their largess. Their businesses needed engineers, who with time came also to fill the ranks of management, but an engineering education in the late nineteenth century fell short of the goals of Jefferson and his followers, or even of Carnegie, and trained engineers turned managers exhibited particular vulnerability to the materialism of their surroundings.

The business elite was recruited in discouraging degree from the children of the elite, children blessed with the advantages of economic security, higher education, and influential friends. Careers in the United States remained more open to talent than they did in any other contemporary society, and relatively poor men of advantageous background and strong character again and again won fortune and fame, but the percentage of those whose parents were farmers or workingmen, and who yet rose past the level of farmers or foremen or clerks, was slowly diminishing. Perhaps on that account, perhaps because of the obvious exceptions to it, the telling of the rags-to-riches story lost none of its old appeal. The autobiographies of Carnegie and Mellon had their counterparts by the hundreds in rude fiction. Again and again Horatio Alger's legendary newsboys built their careers upon the qualities Poor Richard had commended, and always they also profited from some lucky accident, presumptive evidence of the intercession of the Deity.

The consolidators often cast themselves, like Carnegie, as terrestrial substitutes for God. As Christian men, they recognized some responsibility for magnanimity, for a generous stewardship of their wealth. Their charity relieved the most obvious burdens of those whom they considered the worthy poor, and subsidized the cultural activities they deemed most proper.

The daily disbursements of the rich, moreover, had in themselves a broad exemplary effect. The conceits of opulence were constantly displayed in mansions at Newport and Nob Hill, along peacock parades at grand hotels and sumptuous spas, and in growing private hoards of porcelains and jades and precious manuscripts. Henry C. Frick, the Coke King, sometime associate of Carnegie, made himself an emperor among collectors. Advised by connoisseurs of art and its allure to egoism, Frick built a palace on Fifth Avenue where he was wont to sit, high on a Renaissance throne, Van Dyck and Rembrandt near his side, reading *The Saturday Evening Post* while his obliging organist rendered "Silver Threads among the Gold." That pose mocked both prudence and philanthropy. J. P. Morgan's oceangoing yacht or the dinners of the Four Hundred at Delmonico's cost more and registered a clearer impression on the consciousness of most Americans than did a Bowery mission or a public library. For Americans-on-the-make, beguiled spectators at the coliseum where the wealthy played, the promises of stewardship were less compelling than the older promises of Franklin.

No achievement, no creed, no rationalization could relax the tension between the conditions of industrial life and the demands of the cultural heritage. The distribution of industrial plenty left unrewarded many men of talent, character and self-esteem. Average personal real income was rising, but few farmers or unskilled workers acquired much of comfort or convenience. Instead they knew long hours, low pay, grim housing, poor health, and often spiritual desolation. Professional men were better off, but they gained on the average relatively little above their returns of earlier years. The benefits of productivity accrued disproportionately to those who owned or directed production and its organization. The huge fortunes of a few hundred men, the huge luxuries and reputations that they bought, established a degree of contrast of wealth and poverty previously unknown in the United States. Except among the very rich and those who hoped soon to join them, self-respecting men had cause to question the primacy of wealth as a measure of merit, and greater cause to wonder whether poverty revealed sin.

Among the very wealthy, furthermore, though there were exceptions, a preoccupation with getting and having left little room for selfless dedication to exemplary nationhood, little room for innerness or its exultant self-expression, or for rapport with the land and its natural messages. A success that was only material was, as the Emersonians feared, not just crass but also alien to the wholeness of the national ideals. Accordingly not one of the consolidators, not one of the very rich, ever won equivalent place beside the public men who had set and symbolized the mission of America.

☆

For the public itself, industrialists prescribed a restricted role. If wealth was the measure of virtue, most men were wicked or corruptible, and therefore inept judges of the uses of the state. From the angle of the elite, the majority was a beast, and the state could not safely take its guidance from officials chosen by the people. Rather, the commonwealth should be trusted to the wisdom of the successful and to the concatenation of their private competitions and deliberations. Government in this theory had two essential purposes: the restraint of the crowd and its agitators, and the protection of property and its gatherers. Government had a related duty to promote the general welfare by promoting industry, as Hamilton had maintained, but an equal duty to let business go its unimpeded way, as laissez-faire doctrines, well rooted in America, proposed.

It followed that the wealthy had an obligation to remind a public servant if he erred — a duty, if need be, to ease the way to office of candidates who understood their proper function. If the wise and good proved their truth in commerce, as the theory held they did, then politicans were naturally lesser men whose conduct had now and then to be assured by regrettably unwholesome means. In behalf of safe and promotive government, therefore, some of the virtuous stooped unashamed to conquer wicked politicians. Those politicians were then more or less expected to manipulate their corruptible constituents, and when that phenomenon recurred, it was cited as a clinching proof of the premises on which elite political theorists had built. Once more the argument was circular, but plausible if evidence was arranged to fit it.

The growth and patterning of American industrialism owed much to public policies that responded to the argument and tactics of the consolidators. At small cost or obligation to themselves, they obtained large, even crucial, privileges. Some of these were local — liberal franchises for the development of urban services; permissive criteria for incorporation and investment; inexpensive and indulgent government. Some of these were national — a protective tariff; direct subsidies of land or money; free or inexpensive access to timber and mineral resources; a banking and monetary system allowing for private domination; a system of taxation that exacted nothing from the incomes or the fortunes of huge corporations or rich men. Those privileges counted no more than did valuable immunities. Neither the local nor the national governments called the consolidators to significant account for their business procedures, for their operations in the money market, for the quality of their products, for the safety of their employees, or for their treatment of their laboring force.

Those who felt they suffered from government's permissiveness were able now and then to elect sympathetic representatives, but when they mustered sufficient votes to pass remedial legislation, they found the courts committed to the perpetuation of corporate immunity. No other private organizations stood safely, as the corporations did, beyond the bench's interpretation of the law. Yet judges, with singular exceptions, were not the lackeys of the corporations. Rather, they spoke from convictions that coincided with those of the business elite. They had an elite status themselves. Some on the highest federal courts were recruited from among the distinguished members of the bar. More came from politics to the lower courts and were in time promoted. The latter group had ordinarily a vacuous legal education. The apprentice system in which they trained had lost the creative impact of its prewar years. Their advocacy and political experience taught them more of cleverness and partisanship than of judiciousness and jurisprudence. Even law schools in the late century offered largely tired texts and tests of memory and swollen rhetoric.

Lacking the sensitivity and imagination bred by knowledge of law, most judges leaned contentedly upon the more cogent briefs offered in the arguments they heard. This gave a telling influence to the counselors for corporations, the most skillful, the most learned, the best paid members of the bar. To support their clients' cases, they extrapolated from rulings handed down in simpler times, adapting them, though not without distortion, to the legal needs of industry. Though neither bench nor bar were ever of a single mind, a succession of opinions, building gradually on each other, brought the construction of the Constitution into operative harmony with the consolidators' preferences. In so doing, moreover, the federal judiciary, by training and by feeling aligned with "all the forms of associated capital," dressed materialism and elitism in the garments of freedom and the dignity of man.

The federal courts during the 1870's recognized the power of the states to regulate businesses active within their borders, but in the next two decades the Supreme Court erected barriers to the exercise of that authority. By that time constitutional law had defined corporations unequivocally as persons. Now the Court made corporations the primary beneficiaries of the Fourteenth Amendment. That amendment, which had been designed to protect the civil rights of the freed Negroes, forbade the states, as the Fifth Amendment forbade the federal government, to deprive any person of life, liberty, or property without due process of law. Originally due process had referred to procedures, to established practices of trial and legislation. Now, however, the Supreme Court redefined due process in a series of decisions that gave the phrase a substantive meaning. The Court would review not only the conditions under which a regulatory statute was passed but also the content of the statute. Previously the reasonableness of a statute, or of a resulting ruling by an administrative agency, had been deemed a legislative question. Now the Court maintained that due process of law entitled a corporation to a judicial determination of reasonableness.

The Court's new position revealed its grave doubts about the competence of legislatures to govern, about — that is —

one fundamental tenet of democracy. As one influential lawyer put it, legislatures could not be trusted because they were subject to the whims of temporary majorities "inflamed with class-prejudice, envy or revenge." In order to protect property, it behooved the Court, in the words of Mr. Justice Brewer, to "re-write . . . the affirmations of the Declaration of Independence, in language so clear and peremptory that . . . no man, not even a legislator, can misunderstand." For Brewer, the inalienable rights of liberty and the pursuit of happiness put property and industry and the men who managed them beyond the reach of government. That was the basis for broadening the scope of judicial review. The Court was resolved to pass upon the reasonableness of a statute and its enforcement so as to check the impulses, presumed to be corrupt, of the people. Indeed in a decision of 1898 the Court not only reasserted its final authority over reasonableness, in this instance of a rate, but also spelled out the economic principles which legislatures had to follow in determining rates. Those included consideration of the original cost of a corporation's property, of its replacement value, and of the market value and earning capacity of its securities. All these and more were to be given "such weight as may be just and right," and all were subject to the Court's surveillance.

The doctrine of substantive due process also served to prevent legislatures from protecting the welfare of industrial workers. According to another decision of 1898, the liberty of an individual under the Fourteenth Amendment embraced his right to use his faculties as he chose, "and for that purpose to enter into all contracts which may be proper . . . and essential." This liberty of contract, the Court later ruled, gave every laborer the right to work for as many hours each day as he wished, (and by implication for as little pay as he liked). A New York statute limiting the hours of work was therefore found to violate the Constitution.

Where the metaphysics of due process had no relevance, the Court found other ways to endorse the industrial situation. The authority of the federal government over interstate commerce shrank just before the century ended when the Court voided the practice by which the Interstate Commerce Commission had for a decade passed upon the reasonableness of railway rates challenged by a shipper. In 1895 the Court found the refining of sugar outside of commerce. That ruling, which saved a virtual monopoly from conviction under the Sherman Antitrust Act of 1890, occasioned speculation about the utility of the act under almost any circumstances. It apparently applied, as the Court saw it, primarily to labor unions. During a railroad strike of 1894, one union had been successfully enjoined on the basis of the Sherman Act from conspiracy in restraint of commerce. Commending this usage, the *American Law Review* described the strike as a "servile insurrection . . . an attempt to wrest from intelligent and capable men the property they have acquired." The railroads, in contrast to the strikers, "represented the right of every man to manage his own business and to keep his own contracts without dictation." In this description, Jefferson's pursuit of happiness had come to cover not only commercial bargains but also the open shop.

The Court reached a kind of zenith in its decision of 1895 invalidating the federal income tax. The ruling, reversing a clear precedent, found the income tax a direct tax which, according to the Constitution, had to be apportioned among the states on the basis of their populations. That finding converted genuine fears into obstructive law. Eminent counsel, in arguing against the income tax, had equated it with an assault on property, "the very keystone of the arch upon which all civilized government rests." The "passions of the people," he admitted, were "aroused on this subject," but that made it all the more vital that the Court "resolutely and courageously declare . . . that it has the power to set aside an act of Congress violative of the Constitution, and that it will not hesitate . . . no matter what the threatened consquences of . . . populistic wrath."

The spirit of that statement infused the judgments of the Court. It had doubted the competence of legislatures because it distrusted the people. That distrust proceeded largely from bountiful evidence of growing discontent with the patterns and inequities of industrialism. To shield the privileges of industrial wealth and power, the Court, thwarting the clear purpose of a majority of the people, ironically arrogated to its elitist dogma the eloquence of democracy.

Yet the Supreme Court, as Mr. Justice Holmes said in one great dissent, reached its decisions "upon an economic theory which a large part of the country does not entertain," a theory that "has nothing to do with the right of a majority to embody their opinions in law." Like the industrialists, the bar and the bench tended to confuse what Emerson considered the whole moral purpose of the nation with the single goal of economic abundance and the particular instruments that produced it. That confusion derived in part from the friction that had always existed among the values of American culture. The spokesmen for the industrial status quo were by their own lights eliminating that friction by developing a unifying ideology. They did not understand that their ideology, whatever its internal logic, conflicted with ideals that it purported to absorb.

☆

Conservative spokesmen also summoned unifying symbols to the support of their position. One of those symbols was the Constitution itself, not just the document but the prevailing interpretation then revered in the collective name of the Founding Fathers. Some of those interpretations made convenient allowances for the rights of states. But with the memory of the Civil War still fresh, the Union embodied the Constitution's living purpose, and by extension in conservative rhetoric, attacks on any projection of the Constitution's meaning implied attacks upon the Union, un-American attacks. The radical thus became as foreign as the immigrant. This doctrine made Washington the patron of property as well as patriotism, made Jefferson incipiently an anarchist as well as a secessionist, and went on to cleanse Lincoln of Jeffersonian sensibilities. Sentimentality abetted that transmutation, which substituted "homely simple goodness" for Lincoln's passion.

No sentimental hero of the time evoked as much affection as William McKinley. A diligent rather than a clever youth, child of an unpretentious family, McKinley reached manhood before sampling whiskey, tobacco or even ice cream. As a volunteer in the Union army he was brave, for he never imagined he might be killed; he kept neat and accurate records; and he rose through the ranks to a majority. He was also a magnanimous victor, for there was within him a masculine sweetness born of his abiding, suffusing Methodist faith. Charity, one touchstone of that faith, insulated him from prejudices that overcame his Ohio neighbors, and sustained him through his marriage to a vain and selfish woman. Charity also led him, as President, to tolerate senile or inept subordinates. McKinley, Theodore Roosevelt once complained, had "no more back-bone than a chocolate eclair." Soft too on intelligence, he nevertheless moved audiences with a voice as monotonous, as harmonious, as soothing as his ideas. He believed in all the small towns of America, in any Republican platform, in the encouragement of business, and eventually in the divine office of his nation in its missions overseas. With serene confidence, he expected every crisis to resolve itself. So, by and large, did those of his countrymen fortunate enough to remain comfort-able and secure during the depression and the war of the 1890's. They recognized themselves in McKinley, they ap-plauded what they saw, and they identified him with homilies they had learned to recite, with love for kitchen and veranda, for dumb animals and little children. But they left him what he really was, a Franklin without wisdom, a Hamilton without daring, a Washington without majesty. Even in his own day he appeared less distinctive, less powerful, less admirable than Carnegie. For most Americans since that day he has simply disappeared, save as a metaphor of wooden complacency.

☆

Conservative doctrines and expositions convinced few Americans for whom industralism offered suffering rather than satisfactions. West and South, impoverished farmers brought passion to the politics they directed against their supposed tor-menters, against speculators, warehousemen, owners of rail-roads and of the barbed wire "trust," owners of local banks and their correspondent bankers in New York. The fierceness and bitterness of Populism had their equivalents in the violence at Homestead and Pullman, where striking workers rebelled against subsistence wages, callous management, and brutal Pinkertons. The wrath of those and other vivid protests reached proportions that seemed, for brief occasions, almost revolutionary.

Yet even at some peaks of anger, and ordinarily as soon as passions fell, the doctrines of protest found expression not in revolutionary rhetoric but in the American promise. For farmer constituents and others who would listen, agrarian reformers invoked heroic symbols of the past to authenticate the cultural integrity of new proposals for political and economic change.

Western and southern farmers, captives of continual agricultural distress, especially resented the wealth and power and privileges of the consolidators. Jefferson's belief in the common people and his pastoral bias exactly suited the late nineteenth century agrarian mood. Reading history through his eyes, farmer reformers found their "purposes . . . identical with the purposes of the National Constitution." Washington, in their gloss, was a Jeffersonian, and "filled with the spirit of the grand general and chief who established our independence," they sought, they said, "to restore the government of the Republic to the hands of 'the plain people' with which class it originated." So also rustic protest looked for a new Andrew Jackson "to stand, as Jackson stood, against the encroachments of organized wealth." Like the Jacksonians, most farmers at most times in the eighties and nineties held themselves "not enemies . . . of any corporation that will advance our industrial interests . . . We are not enemies to capital, but we oppose the tyranny of monopolies . . . excessive salaries, high rates of interest, and exorbitant . . . profits in trade." The agrarian — indeed the democratic — conception of abundance presumed that wealth would be distributed so as to put the decencies to life within the grasp of every man. "You were born in plenty and spent your childhood in plenty," a farming Daniel told his neighbors, but ". . . the plenteous flow of milk and honey" now passed by, leaving tenants where once had been independent husbandmen. One proper purpose of all government, another rural spokesman said, was "to put rings in the noses of hogs." To that point he cited a letter of Lincoln celebrating Jefferson's birthday, a letter expressing Lincoln's belief "in the man and the dollar, but in cases of conflict . . . in the man before the dollar." And the kinds of men the orator put first were "the attorney in a country town," "the merchant at the cross-roads store," "the farmer who . . . toils all day."

In a similar spirit, labor leaders as the century turned attacked caste and injustice, but not abundance or the tools for its production. "A visitor to a great factory," one said, "may be delighted with the order and system which he observes, but . . . true prosperity is not so much a question of superior production as of . . . more equitable conditions." As another union official put it, the consolidators were reducing the individual "to the condition of a . . . piece of machinery." They were closing to the people, "the rightful owners," the "great fields of opportunity and production." This, he said, was treasonable; it Europeanized the United States; it "absorbed for a greedy few" the "grand inheritance" of America.

That grand inheritance, as Emerson had noted, was middle class, and in its tradition, the farmers and laborers of America directed their major efforts to achieving the best hopes, both material and spiritual, of the middle class. There were, to be

sure, some few who thought they wanted to eradicate industrialism or to socialize it, but their influence was slight. More
sensitive critics, radical intellectuals not least, recognized the
gap between the national situation and national aspirations,
but sensed also the ambiguities inherent in the conglomerate
of American goals. Those ambiguities, constantly revealed in
the use of heroic symbols, past or current, also appeared in the
romance or the artificiality of schemes suggested for social
reconstruction. So it was that Henry George, shrewd in his cri-
tique of economic theory, ardent in his compassion for mankind, proposed in the end only a beguiling panacea that promised high profits, high wages, high standards of living in return
for the single tax that neither labor nor most corporations
would have to pay. Edward Bellamy, devoted to Christian
brotherhood, envisaged after all a distant utopia formed by
combinations of consolidations, purged of rivalry, saturated
with amenities, and governed like an army of cherubims.
Even Henry Demarest Lloyd, who understood far more than
the other two about industrial conditions, put his ultimate
faith no more in devices of control than in the "sweet music of
humanity." For all their fervor, those prescriptions had little
practicability. Similarly, propositions for destroying bigness
neglected to consider that size was both a product and a condition of the ebullient economy, with which very few Americans would have willingly dispensed.

The prerogatives and excesses of the enterprisers, not capitalism or industrialism in themselves, ordinarily disturbed
Americans. Economic growth and institutional stability in
the United States advanced one national purpose but threatened others, and thus impugned the aggregate integrity of
them all. The dialectics of reform, illuminating that threat,

provided grave rejoinders to the texts of industry, bench and bar, and provided also timely reminders of the promises of American life. But memory and dialectics by 1900 were not enough to restore a balance of energies among American values. There was needed, too, a new resolution of group interests, a task primarily for politics, which could express the wholeness of the culture but had instead for thirty years responded largely to the particular needs of industry and industrialists. In that period other interests, other groups of men, their circumstances deeply altered, were seeking social and political identities, and congeries of those identities, apposite to their own expectations of an industrial society. As their search proceeded, they accepted, indeed they often endorsed the economic organization of abundance, the great achievement of American industrialists. But they also still prized what the industrialists had challenged — those "grand views in every direction," the principled heritage of an heroic past.

Chapter

3

☆ ☆ ☆ ☆ ☆

A MIDDLE-CLASS

COUNTRY

"THIS MIDDLE-CLASS COUNTRY," Emerson had said of the United States, had got at last in Lincoln a President of middle-class sympathies, but by 1900 industrialization and urbanization had altered deeply the country Emerson had known. Its extremes of wealth and poverty were more critical than they had been four decades earlier. The sympathies of those at either pole appeared remote from the sympathies that Emerson had seen expressed in Lincoln. So, too, the figure of the President that satisfied the center of American opinion in 1900, the man McKinley and all he represented, suggested little that was Lincolnian. Yet beneath its surfaces American culture retained a vital identity, soon to emerge, with the values and strivings of its best past. For all its polarities, for all its pluralism, American society remained in commanding ways a middle-class society in Emerson's benedictory sense.

☆

In the high prosperity of 1900 the middle class itself, with few dissenters, greeted the century ahead with assurance.

Average annual per capita income in the United States exceeded that in Great Britain, the second richest nation, by more than 25 per cent. The average American adult male, according to one middle-class periodical, shared with a wife and three children a two-story, seven-room house and a cash income of $540 a year if he resided on a farm, of $750 if he lived in a city. He subscribed to two newspapers, one daily and one weekly, and in twelve months smoked twenty pounds of tobacco and swallowed over seven gallons of spirits and seventy-five gallons of beer. *The Independent,* a sturdy bourgeois journal, remarked the failure of the prophecies of Karl Marx. Labor was growing wealthier as real wages advanced along with the proportion of skilled workers in the laboring force. The great consolidations of recent years had altered the role of the middle class, but the increase in the number of holders of shares in large enterprises balanced the displacement of some small businesses. With consolidation, moreover, there arose new opportunities for "becoming rich through the management of the large concerns." The designation "middle class" properly included, in the definition of this survey, "the receivers of a moderate share (say of $1500 to $8000 per annum) of the national income, by whatever means of activity or character of investment." More and more Americans enjoyed the amenities of such an income, as evidenced especially by "the vast increase in the number of families able to pay from $300 to $2000 rental per year." "We may say," *The Independent* concluded, ". . . that the proved betterment of the condition of workers . . . make[s] against the contention of any appreciable decline in the numbers of the middle class, while the persistence in business of the great majority of the independent small producers and distributors, joined with the observed tendencies toward retaining the small capitalist, either as stockholder, manager, or office employee, in the new consolidations, indicate a growth in this class. This indication is confirmed by . . . the constantly augmented demand for middle-class commodities, and . . . is triumphantly supported by the marvelous increase in the number of middle-class houses and apartments."

Yet most Americans had something less or more than the *Independent's* quota for middle-classness. An average annual income of $750 fell by half below the journal's minimum figure for a comfortable standard of living. In a time of heavy, continuing immigration that had in twenty years brought nine million foreigners to the United States, predominantly to the cities, the search for meager lodgings in the spreading slums marked urban life at least as dramatically as did demand for decent housing. Between a third and a half of industrial workers lived in poverty; millions of them, including women and children, worked sixty hours a week or more under despicable conditions and for subsistence wages. Less than a third of American children completed primary school; less than a tenth finished high school. Like the poor, the rich lived beyond the borders of the middle class. The wealthiest 1 per cent owned almost half of the nation's property and received some 15 per cent of its income, many times the $8000 per family per year which, for the *Independent*, marked the upper bourgeois bracket. Still, many of those with more than middle incomes, and many, too, with less, placed themselves and were accepted as members of the middle class.

Income and wealth did not alone measure social status in the United States. Ancestry, for another variable, also mattered. That statistically average American adult male of 1900 had forbears mostly of British but partly of German origin. He usually also had a misinformed conviction of his and their ethnic superiority to men of other races and nationalities. Cutting across lines of wealth, ethnic consciousness sustained a special pride among the economically underprivileged of old American stocks. White dirt farmers, grubby, ignorant, and underfed, long disdainful of Negroes and Indians, considered themselves more important and somehow more pure than immigrants from eastern and southern Europe, including those whose worldly success they resented and suspected. As the volume of immigration rose after 1900, bringing to the United States more and more of the swarthy from the Mediterranean, the Balkan, Baltic and Slavic states, more and more Catholics and Jews, differences of appearance and accent, differences of manner and custom, became more perceptible. Newcomers who acquired the appurtenances of middle-class status did not ordinarily achieve that status in the eyes of those self-defined as an ethnic elite. To that considerable fraction of Americans, the poverty of most immigrants and their children seemed to reinforce the assumption of their inferiority, while that assumption in turn, even when contradicted by achievement, precluded full acceptance of the arriviste.

The Saturday Evening Post, that centrifuge of middle-class taste and values, published during the first half of 1900 some two hundred gossipy sketches of American "Men and Women of the Hour." All were of British or German extraction except for a few Jews and four others with resoundingly Irish names. One of them, a "homeless, orphaned waif" of New York, had "possessed but one name — that of Brady" until a Judge Green of Indiana instructed his wife to "pick out the toughest gamin in the lot" of small children sent west for adoption.

"That was the way," the *Post* reported, intending no irony, that "John Green Brady — the boy took his patron's name — found his way into a Christian home," and later through school and Yale College to a mission in Alaska and ultimately the governorship of that territory. The *Post* and its heroes and heroines consistently felt much less affinity for "foreigners," even those who earned $8000 a year or more, than for poorer farmers and artisans with Yankee pedigrees.

Nevertheless farming and the manual arts, while respectable, lacked the status of unequivocally middle-class occupations. Among the approved occupations, as the *Independent* suggested, were those of self-employed merchants and manufacturers, rentiers, office workers, and business managers. *The Saturday Evening Post* paid more attention to other callings. While listing a dozen industrialists and financiers, all rich, among its "Men and Women of the Hour," it also gave generous space to professional men of modest means, lawyers particularly but also scientists, doctors and engineers, educators, scholars and clergymen. In a pantheon that admitted some Europeans of royal blood, the *Post* assigned its largest American quota to men in public affairs, diplomats, Cabinet ministers, United States Senators, governors, mayors and lesser politicians. Though almost all of that group achieved initial eminence in law or business, public service at sundry levels of authority carried with it notable prestige. Three other kinds of professional men were more remarked than any others save lawyers and politicians: first, authors, editors and publishers; second, actors and musicians; and third, officers in the army, the navy and the national guard. In making its choices, the *Post*, to be sure, was not attempting to establish a social hierarchy. Its concern with the newsworthy, with fame as well as merit, slanted its selections. But its allotments of occupations accorded roughly with the ratios that prevailed in *Who's Who in America*, one prominent directory of middle-class success. Further, just as the *Post* almost omitted those stigmatized by the wrong ancestry, so did it leave out the poor, save for a night watchman at the zoo in Central Park whose quaint task and talents won him condescending mention.

The *Post*'s descriptions of its worthies endowed them with virtues admired by Americans for more than a hundred years, pictured them as popular bourgeois fiction presented its benign protagonists, commended them as examples to its readers. In the *Post*, as in American society, a proper occupation helped to place a man within the middle class. The majority of those so employed demonstrated their status also by the standards of their incomes and their ancestry, and a man who passed all three crude tests displayed a certain social pedigree. Yet no one of the criteria was rigid; each imparted extra flexibility to the others; and even taken together, they still admitted of exception.

☆

To the discomfort of some Americans, but to the auspicious satisfaction of many more, little was fixed about social status in the United States. Continuous movement, up and down, breached the soft edges of the middle class and crossed vague gradations of prestige within it. "Find your own level," one correspondence school exhorted. "Are you wasting your time in a lowly position? . . . Change your occupation. Through courses in . . . Electrical, Mechanical . . . Civil Engineering . . . by mail." "Study law at home," another advertised. ". . . Takes spare time only . . . Improve your condition and prospects." Hard work and self-improvement, the message promised, still brought money and esteem, and in thriving country towns becoming cities, tradesmen's sons, successfully self-taught in law or real estate or engineering, penetrated informal social registers. For a middle class in motion, manners, like riches, set one measure of a man, and manuals of etiquette, in large demand, instructed the uninitiated in gentility. Besides grammatical speech and the right utensils at the table, they needed a large house, placed well away from the depot, acquaintanceship with a city banker, membership in a respected church, a sponsor at the Masonic Lodge or Elks, clean linen, shined shoes, a shaved face and a gold watch. The situation differed only in degree at the frontier of the inner circle in Manhattan. A candidate there, one society matron recommended, needed a house on Fifth Avenue and a summer home at Newport or Bar Harbor, friendship with a European countess, association with a fashionable charity, a patroness to solicit important invitations, and a feminine ability "to touch hidden chords of sentiment . . . to charm, to lighten care." On the escalator of the middle class, the prudential virtues at the basement vanished in the courtly graces of the roof.

The prudential virtues took their classic place with other principles the middle class still honored. For much of that class, the nation remained the public, collective, transcendant embodiment of private, individual good character. Honorable service in responsible office, civilian or military, guaranteed prestige and middle income, and at once rewarded achievement and enhanced future opportunity. Among the "strong young men" of Washington in 1900, as *The Saturday Evening Post* described them, was Perry Sanford Heath, who had worked and saved since, as a printer's devil at age thirteen, he earned a dollar and a half a week and put his surplus out on loan at interest. For some years a newspaper correspondent, Heath had become Assistant Postmaster General, appropriately within the executive department Benjamin Franklin had first dignified. Frank Arthur Vanderlip, Assistant Secretary of the Treasury, passed from an apprenticeship in a machine shop to typesetting to a financial newspaper and then to government, from which he admittedly looked ahead, a young Hamilton, to commercial and investment banking in New York. David Jayne Hill, Assistant Secretary of the Department of State, once Jefferson's department, had proved his truth pursuing knowledge. While a freshman at college, though two years deficient in Greek, he had insisted on enrolling in the standard course in which he scored a grade of ninety-five. In all his undergraduate years he never missed a meal, never cut a class, and once forewent a fancy suit of clothes in order to spend a $60 prize on an encyclopedia. And Lieutenant J. Lee Hall, Thirty-third United States Infantry in the Philippines, like "Old Hickory" a "synonym . . . for courage," won national notice for clearing DeWitt County, Texas, of a band of desperadoes preying on the farmers who had settled with their families on the open prairie there.

In contrast to those of the *nouveaux riches* who turned from work and thrift to lavish spending, the diplomats and soldiers, in the model roles the *Post* assigned them, committed their reputations to honor, service and restraint. Those aristocratic qualities, dear to Brooks Adams and other descendants of the ruling American families of the late eighteenth century, lay at the core of the curricula that the eastern seaboard colleges presumed to teach. They also appealed to magazines popular with the middle class when the twentieth century began, among them the *Post,* the *Independent,* the *Outlook, Harper's Weekly,* the *American Review of Reviews,* the *Atlantic, St. Nicholas* and *Youth's Companion.* In their pages they treated the imaginative virtues, including those of the poet and artist, with a banality Adams loathed, but their respect for honor and service was no less than his. Rather, their respect for sheer wealth was usually much more. Middle-class periodicals, whether reflecting, reinforcing or shaping middle-class opinion, endorsed middle-class aspirations for two kinds of success, the success of the market place and the success of virtue. Gradations of status within the middle class rested now on one, now on the other, now on both kinds of success, and middle-class men disagreed about which more to seek or to applaud. But so long as both were potentially available, as in 1900 in some degree they were, to men of relatively low incomes, relatively unknown families, and relatively undistinguished occupations, movement upward in social status remained beguiling, except perhaps for several score like Adams who preferred their virtuous aloneness at the top.

Yet others, born to Adams's standing or to great wealth, gave themselves to public service and directed their service to enhance the opportunities for a rising middle class. Indeed men of patrician and men of affluent origins tended to converge on similar goals. By 1900 families of proper Bostonians, who knew the Adamses well, had been accumulating wealth assiduously for three generations and were displaying it with quiet elegance along shores from York to Falmouth. Their emulators in Cleveland, Minneapolis and San Francisco copied more than their manners. Like Boston's Saltonstalls and Lodges the new rich frequently sought high public office, often at first in order to possess a grand title or to protect a vulnerable interest, but often also, especially in a second generation with unselfish *richesse oblige*. Indeed by 1900 a few of the second generation of multimillionaires, like some of the less wealthy middle class, had begun to deny the elitist doctrine, so treasured among the consolidators, that made innate shiftlessness the source of poverty. Moved partly by the religion of sweet humanity, partly by the Darwinian logic that emphasized the force of nurture over nature, partly by the comprehension of previously unknown data about the problems of the poor, a resolute minority of the middle class believed the indigent entitled to a larger share of American opportunity and abundance. Some men of that mind intended by elevating the mass to separate them from the baleful influence of the rich, while some hereditary millionaires, no less or more high-minded, dedicated their fortunes to making their influence benign. If a sense of guilt about their comforts motivated both groups, so did their belief in the desirability and deservedness of a society that rewarded talent and character wherever they appeared.

Accordingly the philanthropy of even the new rich followed courses earlier delineated by such as the Adamses and earlier exemplified in the symbols of Franklin and Jefferson. The thirty-four largest gifts to public causes in 1899, in all some $80 million, allotted a major share to education — over $55 million to institutions of higher learning, over $5 million to libraries, and almost $3 million to museums. Those figures, the *Independent* noted, "show . . . that we are beginning to recognize that men of wealth have an obligation . . . to do good with their money . . . It is sometimes said that it is a disgrace for a Bostonian to die without a bequest to Harvard College. Something of the same feeling now extends over the country." Gifts for education in the morning of the twentieth century benefited colleges and universities throughout the United States, grade and high schools in the South — the neediest section — and special institutions for those American untouchables, the Negroes and Indians. The gifts were not entirely altruistic, for a munificent donor immortalized himself, and the middle class in all gradations believed that collegiate or professional education, especially at a renowned university, enlarged a young man's chances for a socially salutary career. Both the patricians and the middle class also considered education useful for spreading their values to the poor. But a corollary dictum expected education to equip the deserving of any class or race or nationality for eventual social movement. So it was that *Harper's Weekly* pointed to "the contrast between the primitive native and the neat, tidy children" attending a new school for Indians. "Original sin may be ineradicable," the magazine granted, "but education seems in a fair way to remove the aboriginal king." With similar optimism the *Independent* found enlightenment in yellow journalism: "The proletary, the mudsill, the clodhopper . . . has learned to read, and takes the daily paper . . . This is the greatest wonder of the age . . . He is reading and so is thinking . . . You can't tell how far a man will go when he sets out."

Wherever he wanted to go, some of the middle class were prepared to assist and receive, others to restrain and exclude him. The insecurities endemic in a fluid society battled with its more generous, democratic impulses. Those insecurities accounted for anxieties about social status that characterized every American social group —the aspiring among the poor who drove themselves and their children mercilessly toward polite respectability; the uneasy among the rich who knew the social perils of financial failure or lapsed gentility; and especially the jealous among the middle class who felt themselves overshadowed from above by great wealth and threatened from below by the assertive van of a surging, alien mass. Yet for three generations similar anxieties had troubled Americans, alike in periods of quiet and periods of contest, without uniting the middle class even briefly in support either of change or of the status quo, without ever wholly erasing middle-class prescriptiveness and without ever fixing it rigidly.

☆

Probably no one better displayed at once the prescriptiveness and the permissiveness of the middle class than did Theodore Roosevelt, the strongest young American of the turn of the century. In 1900 Governor of New York and Republican Vice-Presidential candidate, Roosevelt had a flair for robust heroics. His hunting trips as a Dakota rancher, now for bears, now for outlaws; his recruitment and command of the boisterous Rough Riders; his staccato energy and symbolic white sombrero — all colored, without concealing, his patrician birth and breeding. To his detractors in the world of business, who recognized his hostility to their commercial ethic, he seemed, as one of them said, "a damned cowboy," but nothing rural or radical or uncouth affected Roosevelt's social views. Henry George, Demarest Lloyd and William Jennings Bryan seemed Jacobins to him, and he deplored their sinister influence on the susceptible mob, "the slow, obstinate farmer," "organized labor in the lowest unions," the "crooks" and "criminals." He also associated that susceptibility with the Irish and other inferior "races," by which he meant the peoples of southern and eastern Europe. They fell naturally into the political party and the occupations he scorned. "There were," he had observed of his colleagues in the New York Assembly, "six liquor sellers, two bricklayers, a butcher, a tobacconist, a pawnbroker, a compositor and a typesetter . . . all Democratic; but of the farmers and lawyers, the majority" were Republicans. Above all, Roosevelt despised the *noveaux riches* and "the people of good family" like them, who "took little interest in literature or politics . . . did not care to explore or hunt . . . put wealth above everything else, and therefore hopelessly vulgarized their lives."

Yet Roosevelt was neither aloof nor pessimistic. His personal friends, let alone his political associates, included Catholics and Jews, Latins and Slavs, railroad vice-presidents, union leaders, and at least one obstinate and homicidal cowpoke. Whatever their fortunes, whatever their origins, whatever their callings, men could commend themselves to Roosevelt, as he said, by their "self-restraint and courage and hard work, and careful training in mind and in the manly virtues." Further, while he did not ordinarily admire impoverished or unlettered men, Roosevelt insisted that they deserved assistance. "The sphere of the state's action" needed to be "vastly increased," he argued, as a first step toward a community of the future rid of extremes of wealth and poverty, a middle-class community.

That vision of their community endlessly extended at some point in time between urgency and eternity was a dominant vision of the American middle class. They disagreed among themselves about the ways to achieve it, about its eligible membership, about the ratio within it of creature comforts to personal character. To those questions most middle-class men in 1900 would probably, like Roosevelt, have proposed ambiguous answers. The middle class held a sense of general identity, a calculus of income and family and occupation and manner that many of its members usually interpreted strictly. But it also retained a sense of values, drawn from the past and pertinent to the future, that persuaded some within its ranks occasionally to stretch their standards for identification to include potentially all who qualified, all who were virtuous. That was enough to keep middle-class society open, enough to encourage outsiders to attempt to acquire credentials for getting in.

☆

Aspiration to middle classness, and therefore receptivity to middle-class values with all their ambiguities, tinged American subcultures that were otherwise heterogeneous. In cities, suburbs and villages, to Yankees and Germans, Swedes, red Indians and Italians, children's primers conveyed only middle-class lessons and pictures. Americans, whatever their backgrounds, learned a middle-class vocabulary if they learned to read. If they found it irrelevant to everything else they knew, they might resist or reject it, but with few exceptions, they could discover some exegesis, some social slang, that confirmed while also vulgarizing dubious language in the text. Within or close to almost every grimy neighborhood, the experience of some one or some few men ratified the possibility of advancement, established human models of accredited deportment, and equipped them to furnish patronage to their protégés.

American farmers had never lost their conception of their own middle-classness. Indeed much of the rural protest that

Theodore Roosevelt called radical expressed a proper resentment against loss of income and independence, for which most farmers blamed the industrial consolidators, their beneficiaries and their allies. Yet even at the zenith of agrarian discontent, the angry wanted less to revolutionize the economy than to restore conditions they considered optimum for their own purposes and esteem. Rising land values and commodity prices in the early years of the twentieth century, relieving distress and softening tempers, dispelled some rural nostalgia, but farmers were then no less intent than they had been on reaffirming their social position. The prevalence of commercial agriculture continued to fix much of their energy on sheer economic gain. In some cases a kind of rustic gentry asserted its status in acres of land, herds of cattle, bales of cotton or bushels of wheat — and the thousands of dollars these displayed. The counselors of the less successful stressed the importance of increasing production by efficient and scientific agriculture, and of adopting businesslike methods for marketing crops. Those counterparts to the practices of industrial management would assure larger profits which in turn promised "comfort and social advantages . . . and a good . . . life on the farm."

The components of that proposed good life resembled the social advantages common to the urban middle class: sound medicine and sanitation; good schools and colleges offering both general and professional curricula; complex machines and appliances for saving labor on the job and drudgery in the home; easy communication among people of similar leisure tastes, with art, music and literature in the offing and sociability, worship and fraternity in the main. Perhaps most important, the promotion of middle-class life on the farm would reduce the lure of the city to rural youth, would confirm and uphold the dignity of farming as an occupation. In that goal a Jeffersonian bias was accommodated to an industrial and urban culture. Advocates of the accommodation believed that the well-being of the nation depended in part on the material and moral welfare of its farmers and on the preservation of the kinds of values that Jefferson had associated with the satisfactions of living on the land. Those advocates, influential both in and beyond rural society, were ordinarily themselves identifiable both as farmers or farmers' sons and as typically upper middle-class Americans, particularly as editors and publishers of agricultural journals, instructors and administrators at agricultural colleges, and elected or appointed public officers of high rank. Their dual identities made them conspicuous examples of precisely the accommodation that they preached.

As one method of leadership for agriculture, they relied confidently upon the force of familiar example, their own not least. That force supplied the energy for the demonstration program of Seaman A. Knapp, sometime editor, teacher and college president, whose techniques won the sponsorship of the United States Department of Agriculture and the Rockefeller Foundation. Knapp and his hundreds of agents went directly to dirt farmers in run-down districts, guaranteed to one farmer in each area all the profits and no loss from the experiment they proposed, and gave him detailed instructions for planting, cultivating, crop rotation, diversification and other essentials of scientific agriculture. The gains resulting from his demonstration converted doubting neighbors into eager imitators who were often spurred on by their children, members of local clubs of agronomy that Knapp promoted.

Through other kinds of associations, the Farmers' Union, a Rotary of the countryside, showed its adult membership the benefits of cooperative marketing. Where crops improved and profits rose, farmhouses received new coats of paints and farmers' families new clothes. Through imitative self-improvement, rural men and women of the hour were establishing themselves materially as members of the middle class. In consonance with the moral spirit of middle-class traditions, they were regaining, too, their hope and independence and self-respect.

Thousands of farmers lagged behind, some temporarily, others indefinitely. The latter included most tenants and croppers and migrant workers whose attainments and expectations left them at the bottom of rural society. Many of them moved along to the mills and shanties of urban America. There they were at least potentially better off than they had been, for an efficient agriculture could support only a decreasing number of Americans with decency, and refugees from the land, in spite of their continuing destitution, now and then found in the cities some opportunity for their children. Indeed in the cities, rather more generally than on the land, the possibilities of hopeful emulation were continually lifting new ranks to the middle class.

☆

After five decades and more within the United States, the Catholic Irish in 1900 still felt their separateness. The first of the large group of immigrant strangers to nineteenth-century America, they were still enduring the poverty and prejudice that all later groups of strangers also had to endure. They lived in the cities, mostly among their own, mostly in shabby neighborhoods, in Boston where the Yankees treated them with undisguised contempt, in New York, Chicago, San Fran cisco and elsewhere where the Protestant mood was not much more tolerant. Mostly they held shabby jobs, many of them on construction gangs, on docks, in breweries and mines. Yet by 1900 the Irish in America had an identifiable middle class within their own community, that middle class was growing, and as it grew, it identified itself increasingly with the general middle class. The ethnic separateness of the Irish was being transcended, albeit slowly, without being submerged, as the successful among them entered middle-class occupations, earned middle-class incomes, copied middle-class behavior, and absorbed middle-class values.

For the Irish, as for other immigrant groups, not all careers in America were equally open to men of talent and character. At the turn of the century they had negligible access to senior positions in the management of major corporations, partner- ships in major law firms, senior commands in the armed serv- ices, professorships and presidencies in major universities. Their chances were much larger in other callings that led to the sanction of respectability, especially in the performing arts, the church, and politics. Their own communities needed the services of those occupations. Native minstrels had long relieved their neighbors' cares with Irish songs and Irish stories sung or told in Irish barrooms and Irish music halls. Some of the gifted performers graduated to the American stage where the Irish, once objects for buffoonery, gradually enriched the whole milieu. In the early twentieth century, successful Irish- American actors and entertainers, authors and producers still often gathered in coveys of their own. Now these were here and there adorned in the comfort and the fashion of the

Lambs' Club. Further, the Lambs and others like them were lionized outside of the Irish community as well as within it, and welcome wherever the theater and its folk merged with society at large. By then, the American middle class was acclaiming the tunes and lyrics of George M. Cohan, the Irish son of a performing Irish family, an intimate of public as well as theatrical men, a resident when he chose to be of satisfied suburbia, in his own and other eyes, a Yankee-doodle-dandy.

Similarly, Irish priests had long ministered to their parishioners in terms familiar and beautiful and heartening to them, terms strange and vulgar and even threatening by the standards of their Protestant neighbors. Some of those priests helped to found parochial schools and colleges that preserved for those of the Irish laity who could afford them an intellectual and moral environment the Catholic Church approved, while also creating a channel of training in the mind and the professions then otherwise inadequately open to Catholics. Some of those priests gained advancement within their church to positions as archbishops or cardinals. Among them a notable fraction, without compromising either faith or dignity, represented secular as well as religious values sanctioned by patrician Protestants. The separate definitions of the good life, the good man, the good American of James Cardinal Gibbons, Archbishop John Ireland, and Father John Ryan were essentially the definitions also of Theodore Roosevelt and like-minded strong young men. The eminence, the command, the visible and acknowledged virtue of Cardinal Gibbons especially symbolized the potentialities of the Irish in America. He was exceptional, to be sure, but so, in their different ways, were Lincoln and Carnegie exceptional, so were they models of possibilities. All three were models for all Americans, in-

cluding Irish Catholics, of whom some aspired to archbishop-
rics, some to wealth, some to distinguished public service. A
Roman Catholic, Roosevelt predicted, would become President before the century was old.

There were already dozens of Irish officeholders, mayors,
aldermen, state legislators, precinct captains. Like those who
accompanied or were to follow them in squalid urban wards,
the Irish responded to the calculated compassion of politicians
who made their city machines crude prototypes of social service agencies. By providing a bucket of coal, a Thanksgiving
turkey, a chowder party, a wedding or a bath, ward politicians
gave those they helped a sense of belonging. At once they
evoked the loyalty of their constituents and whetted their
taste for comfort. Trading sporadic benevolence for constant
partisanship, politics assisted the voluntary associations of the
poor, organized to afford mutual protection against loneliness,
disease and death. City politicians defended the saloons, poor
men's clubs, and the privileged corporations, railroads, utilities
and others, who repaid their debts in direct donations of
money and indirect gifts of employment for the faithful and
their families. The system operated through networks of
fealty and homage that drew in the talented, used them, rewarded them, and promoted them to places where their authority and their ambitions intersected with those of the business elite.

George Washington Plunkitt of Tammany Hall, pursuing
wealth and fame and power like his fellow sachems, summed
the whole thing up: "I seen my opportunities and I took 'em."
Politics was a business for Plunkitt. He did the necessary errands, got out the necessary vote, served the necessary apprenticeship that put him within reach of "honest graft" — of lush

contracts for construction of city streets and sewers, of early, inside information about real estate the city planned to buy. Plunkitt succeeded, as he boasted, by accepting the favors he received in return for the favors he offered the residents of his district: "quarters for them . . . clothes for them . . . a job for a deservin' man" and candy for "the children — the little roses . . . the best kind of vote-getters." In Boston "Honey Fitz" Fitzgerald exercised a tough, alert generosity like Tammany's in New York. In Jersey City "Little Bob" Davis distributed dollar bills to the grateful he met on his morning stroll from home to headquarters. In Chicago "Bathhouse John" Coughlin and "Hinky-Dink" Kenna ruled the juiciest tenderloin on the continent where on one occasion they hired a special train to carry the faithful to a rowdy holiday in Colorado, a thousand miles away. At the races at Saratoga Springs, New York, Coughlin appeared in the most resplendent waistcoats and the most inharmonious hues polite society had ever seen. These were the raiments of his pride, the comic, pitiable bunting of assertive status. The owners of the winning stables despised the interloper whose Chicago neighbors adored him for showing his flag and theirs, for proving that one of their own was extravagantly opulent. "Bathhouse John" had kindred spirits in the prize ring where John L. Sullivan and "Gentleman Jim" Corbett testified to Irish prowess and then dressed the part of the champions they were, as did the Irish jockeys and the Irish stalwarts of baseball's National League. Gladiators and consuls, splendid together, exhibited the success of the Irish in copying, indeed in matching, the garish standards of new wealth.

Along the avenues of politics the Irish were also passing more exacting tests. They had much to overcome. The political boss usually preferred not to hold elective office, for public office was exposed, vulnerable to electoral whims, even to political reform. He arranged instead for worthy lieutenants to gather the titles he declined. Enmeshed in the system, they were permissive toward it. Like the charity of the bosses, the politics of their mayors, governors and legislators for many years appeased poverty but did not attack it at the roots. By 1900 time and office-holding had had remedial effects. The generation of Irish-Americans then growing up had begun to believe themselves and their children entitled to the amenities and opportunities that politics provided only partially and irregularly. Accustomed to office-holding, they saw that government could help them to obtain better housing, employment and education. Some were beginning to associate the privilege of office-holding with the responsibility of public service. Departure from the mores of machine politics was neither abrupt nor complete, nor was there soon to be an equivalent of Cardinal Gibbons in public life, but among the strong young men of Irish politics in America there emerged models and champions for a growing, self-conscious, identifiable, unseparated middle class.

Joseph Patrick Tumulty was just old enough to vote when the century turned. The grandson of an immigrant, he remembered an uncle who, after riding with the Union cavalry and later the Pony Express, clothed himself in buckskin, moustache and goatee, a Davey Crockett with a brogue. More vividly he remembered his childhood in the "horseshoe" along the railroad tracks of Jersey City where Bob Davis reigned. There the boy Tumulty perceived the criteria of respectability. His father, a grocer, prospered within the Irish neighborhood as a contractor and dealer in real estate, profiting in his ventures from acquaintanceship with Davis, who twice endorsed his candidacy for the state assembly. The Tumultys displayed their upward march, as did the Yankees on Jersey City's "Heights," in the impressiveness of their successive homes. The first was utterly plain; the second, built upon a basement; the third, equipped also with a porch. The boy Joe played now at applying imaginary white paint to his father's fence, now at moving houses to attractive sites. Mostly he played at politics. "I was a great little parader," he recalled. "One night . . . I walked beside the carriage in which my father was riding . . . All the time I wasn't admiring my father's high hat I was . . . thinking what a grand thing it would be to be in the legislature." A painted fence, a silk hat, a public office — those were ambitions approved in both the "Horseshoe" and the "Heights," and in the prairies and the cotton country, too.

For young Tumulty the track to fulfillment lay partly along approved lines of school and college and training in the law. Though his schools were Catholic, their curricula contained much of the subject matter that was supposed to educate young Protestants at Princeton for the nation's service. His law firm was also Catholic, but the case books in its library were identical to those in use throughout America. Tumulty parted from the lines the middle class endorsed only for his apprenticeship in politics, running errands for the local boss. Yet he accepted the demands of partisanship and personal loyalty without making them his career. Filled with "passionate resentment" over Carnegie's treatment of his striking workers, moved also by the remonstrations and humanity of Henry George and Bryan, Tumulty interpreted "the attempt by eastern financial interests to dominate the Government of the United States" as the "great moral issue" of his day. With half a dozen young Irish-American friends, he joined campaigns for better schools and parks and playgrounds, for subjecting local corporations to state controls and higher taxes, for making local government more responsive to the needs of the whole electorate. "Joe," Bob Davis complained, "I could make you Mayor of Jersey City if you'd only behave." Instead, as a member of the state assembly, Tumulty compiled a voting record basically indistinguishable from those of reforming representatives of middle-class suburbs. The grocer's son, an Alger hero of a sort, owed his success in part to his democratic faith.

It recommended him to Woodrow Wilson who as Governor of New Jersey and later President of the United States made Tumulty his secretary. The first Irish-American to hold an influential White House post, Tumulty stood out as a favorite target of those Protestants who still deemed high office their exclusive preserve. His rank also heightened the expectations of his fellow Irish. So, too, while his fascination and adroitness with the sheer machinery of politics never flagged, he also made a responsible mark on large questions of policy. "I am proud of my Irish blood," he wrote. ". . . I am, however, an American before I am an Irishman." He might have said "a middle-class American." And he was not alone. Several years his senior, Alfred E. Smith overcame greater obstacles to accomplish even more. Governor of New York before Tumulty left office, Smith during the ensuing decade enlarged and projected the example embodied in Tumulty's career. The bigotry they met left its scars on both men, as it did on others like them, but they did not try to show their status in purple waistcoats or to hide their ancestry in gray conformity. Rather, without denying their Irishness, they testified to its compatibility with American ideals.

☆

Like the Irish, Scandinavian- and German-Americans followed careers available to them toward acculturation. Their successful farmers and tradesmen, churchmen, musicians and athletes, beer barons, iron mongers and politicians now reared the scrubbed children of diffident gentility, now flashed the ostentation of sudden wealth, now confirmed the hardiness of democratic virtues. At every level of accomplishment, their ways stamped a pattern for their successors from parts of Europe east and south of Germany. In Jersey City shrewd Robert Davis had Tumulty learn Italian in order to defend new neighbors hailed into local courts. There and elsewhere, in politics and other callings, too, the leaven of social possibility began to raise the strongest to the surfaces of their own communities and thence toward accessibility to the expanding middle class.

Different groups, reflecting different European backgrounds, discovered different blocks and different outlets within the United States. The Jews, for one, peddlers in Prague, were peddlers first but often merchants later in Baltimore and Pittsburgh. They soon dominated the clothing industry, soon built up apartheid banks and brokerage offices, and continually pointed their young toward professions based upon extended education. Some of those professions provided vestibules for others higher on the social ladder. So with Jews, as with the other newcomers, a tailor's or a cobbler's son, blocked by the restrictiveness of medical and law schools or by the paucity of his family's means, might struggle to master dentistry or bookkeeping and then push his sons or nephews to surgery or chancery. And with the Jews, as with the others, the upward climb ordinarily led through the plateaus of vulgar emulation, not around them. In contrast to the Irish and the Italians, the Jews as a group tended for a time to shun politics, but not the prestige or the responsibilities of high office, or the status and satisfactions of formal charity and social work. Jews from eastern Europe, moreover, new to America when the century began, found visible heroic models of a kind among the German Jews who had preceded them, men such as the brothers Nathan, Isadore and Oscar Straus, merchants extraordinary, of whom the last in 1906 became the first of his religion to receive a cabinet appointment; the brothers Irving and Herbert Lehman, born to finance, soon to serve respectively as judge and governor; their friend Henry Morgenthau, creator of his own competence in real estate, in 1913 named ambassador to Turkey; and Louis D. Brandeis, preeminent in law and in social reform, in 1916 the first Jew to reach the United States Supreme Court. Those men worked at times with Tumulty and Smith, with Theodore Roosevelt and Woodrow Wilson. They were models not for Jews only but for all Americans actually or potentially identified with Emerson's kind of middle class.

Prospects for middle-classness were statistically poorer than the examples of a Smith or a Straus suggested. The statistics, however, were still uncompiled, and new Americans were bothered only when they felt their disadvantages within their own experience, in exclusions they confronted or bigotry they observed. Persisting deep into the twentieth century, ethnocentric prejudices erupted now and then in chains of afflictive episodes. Constantly a hierarchy of prejudice set Germans and Irish against each other, or both against Italians, Poles or Greeks. Those who had achieved enhanced status as often banned as helped the men below them. Even the labor movement, middle class in its mood, was little less contemptuous toward the unskilled, little less indifferent to their needs, than was management itself. Within the crafts unions, where by 1900 German, Irish and Jewish Americans exercised much of the leadership, ethnic and status selfishness operated as palpably as it did within Boston and Philadelphia banks.

Yet the very obstacles to mobility dramatized the examples of those who surmounted them. Furthermore, whatever the relative deceleration in social mobility, the absolute growth of opportunity in a prosperous and expanding economy overbalanced it. While that growth usually moved through segregated channels, through Irish partnerships or Jewish stores or Italian banks, it also proceeded in integrated circumstances, and even segregated opportunities brought those who recognized them closer to identification with the general middle class, itself more and more a composite of men of varying religious faiths and family origins. Accordingly the uncommon men who emerged from the obscurity of immigrant communities still lifted the expectations of their fellows. In the sense of possibilities and expectations, the middle class by 1900 stretched far beyond the boundaries drawn by *The Saturday Evening Post*. The American middle class had been always in a state of motion; it was comprehensible also as a proliferating state of mind.

☆

There were strangers to that state of mind and to the temperament and conditions inviting accession to it. Those outsiders were either actively hostile to society and its values or wholly passive, "ox-like, limp and leaden-eyed" in deep defeat. Hopelessness led a fraction of the poorest industrial workers to escapes in reveries about their homelands, or in alcohol, or in madness or in resignation to encroaching death. Alienation moved another, tougher fraction to re-migrate. Bitterness and confusion prompted a segment of the activists to the vengeance and notoriety of crime. Another angry segment supplied the spare ranks of radicalism, of the tiny Socialist Labor Party, the anarchists, the Second International with their revolutionary creeds. Membership in those cadres, numerically insignificant, was preponderantly alien. Indeed the Socialist Labor Party spent much of its small energy in debate with the Socialists who were in the United States markedly middle class in their origin and manner, and in their meliorative, Christian, often utopian, outlook. The most formidable radical organization, the syndicalist Industrial Workers of the World, flourished among immigrant laborers subject to the most wretched conditions of work and ignored by the crafts unions. Taken together, the hopeless and the hostile constituted an inconsequential threat to the stability of American society, but the threat might have materialized had the polarities of society become inflexible; had the possibilities for advancement to the middle class lost their plausibility and allure. Uneasiness about radicalism quickened the sensitivities of much of the middle class, established and emerging, to the attractions of distributing opportunity more broadly. Such sensitivities, along with the jealous insecurities of a fluid society and the magnanimous national view of a good life, turned those who harbored them away from the consolidators and their doctrines and back toward the Lincoln symbol and its message.

Ironically, that message was only rarely interpreted any longer as bearing upon the most rejected 12 per cent of Americans, the non-whites, Negroes in particular. Custom and law removed them from the middle class and access to it. As a group they earned the smallest incomes, suffered the severest ostracism, worked in the meanest occupations, received the worst educations, and competed for the narrowest opportunities. Still largely resident in the South where they subsisted almost entirely as menials or tenant farmers, the Negroes were often no poorer than the white croppers who tilled abutting lands, but precisely because those neighbors were white, they clung to a system of caste based on color that gave them a fatuous but compensatory sense of superior status. Indeed the alienation and anger that poor whites had vented in the protest movements of the 1890's, movements which enlisted Negroes in a common cause, were expressed after 1900 largely in hostility toward Negroes. When whites and Negroes fled rural for urban slums, prejudice and segregation moved with them, infesting the allocation of employment, housing, schooling, transportation, and facilities for leisure, most patently in the cities of the South but effectively also in the North. The Southern white, moreover, like the white immigrants from Europe, had a middle class of his own color to envy, perhaps, but also to emulate; the Negro middle class, in contrast, was less affluent and more submissive.

The dominant Negro leadership when the century turned, a leadership the white community sanctioned, had yet to recommend, much less to expect, middle-class status for Negroes. Booker T. Washington, son of a slave, head of an industrial school for Negroes in Alabama, solicited the assistance of Southern industrialists and Northern philanthropists for a program that acquiesced in Negro disfranchisement and segregation for an indefinite future. "We shall prosper in proportion as we learn to dignify and glorify common labor," Washington maintained. ". . . It is at the bottom of life we must begin . . . The agitation of questions of social equality is the extremist folly." Washington sought for his race training in the manual skills, "the opportunity to earn a dollar in a factory," the chance for the compliant inferiority of the permanent artisan class of Europe, whose fixed status the American promise had rejected as long ago as Franklin. Yet Washington believed, with good reason, as did almost all his contemporaries, that he was seeking for the Negro the most society would deliver in his time. While he also believed that the Negro would eventually prove his right to full social equality, Washington's decision to await rather than to assert that right, differentiated him and the Negroes whose attitude he exemplified from the leaders of white minorities and their flocks.

Negroes and other non-whites, however, were not necessarily the submissive captives of inferiority. The century was still very young when W. E. B. Du Bois, a Northern Negro intellectual, began to organize the agitation Booker Washington deplored. Along with the Negroes who joined him were middle-class whites resolved to keep the national promise not because they were frightened or insecure or guilty, but because they believed in it and in fulfilling it with all deliberate speed. Their spark, and the impressive gains of every other ethnic group, would in time fire the Negro first to recognize and then to demand his proper identity as an American.

☆

Consciousness of American identity with all its connotations ramified through the gradations of social status. It was

as American as the Founding Fathers, after all, to measure esteem in wealth; as American as the Jacksonian enterpreneurs
to spend wealth lavishly; as American as Hamilton to relate
wealth to national strength. But American identity, middle-
class identity, meant more than that, as it always had. Men in
every gradation of the middle class, though not all men or
even most men, however anxious about their relative social
reputation, were also glad in the openness and the heritage of
their society. So Theodore Roosevelt made politics and power
his vehicles for personal fame and national merit. So John D.
Rockefeller, Jr., committed his reputation and his riches
through philanthropy to the realization of values symbolized
in heroic figures of the past. So Seaman Knapp and Tumulty
and Brandeis and Du Bois pointed themselves and their confident imitators toward common goals. There stood aside only
the alienated poor and the imperceptive rich, those abject in
material defeat and those arrogant in material victory, those
without prospects or hope and those without generosity or
faith. The latter were no more distant than the former, but
they were more conspicuous, more influential, more obstruct-
ing of the purposes that kept the middle class in motion and
informed its state of mind. Wealth suited a middle-class
country, but plutocracy did not, any more in 1900 than in Emerson's day. In the ensuing decades, in its manifold ways, a
middle-class country would vent its hopes and hostilities in
middle-class politics again.

Chapter

4

☆ ☆ ☆ ☆ ☆

TO RESTORE THE
ANCIENT TRUTHS

THE SENATOR one Sunday afternoon was engaging in the mildly vexing exercise of meeting the press. "How do you stand on conservation, Senator?" an inquisitor asked. The senator fidgeted. "Well, I tell you," he said. "Some of my constituents are for conservation, and some of my constituents are against conservation, and I stand foursquare behind my constitutents." The inquisition moved on; there was no heresy here. The function of representative government was, after all, to represent; the function of politics, to reconcile peacefully conflicting parochial and particularistic interests.

In the United States during the six decades after 1900 politics continually provided one medium for the difficult adjustment of the American people to advancing industrialism, one process for the conciliation needed to modulate the antitheses of American life. Control of the state when the century turned was a protection for those who had what they wanted, a potential corrective for those who felt themselves deprived. Only positive and imaginative government could perpetuate the national legacy, could preserve the conditions essential to economic abundance while restoring the conditions essential to human dignity and to freedom.

☆

In meeting what they took to be the realities of corporate life, American industrialists by 1900 had excited a growing resistance from other groups. Farmers, for one, suspicious in any case of industrialism and urbanism, had special grievances and objectives. They had long urged government control or even ownership of the railroads, maintaining that the policies of private management placed an inequitable burden on agricultural commodities. They advocated also public or cooperative ownership or control of grain elevators and other crop warehouses. This, the argument went, would reduce the cost of marketing crops and permit the farmer to hold produce for high prices, to reap for himself the speculative gains which were accruing to owners of elevators and operators in futures. The capitalistic predilection inherent in those demands revealed itself also in the farmers' attitude toward money. By the use of one device or another, they wanted an increase in the supply of money and a decrease in the cost of credit; an inflation in the prices their products commanded, a deflation in the prices of goods and services they used. So too in thinking about the tariff or taxation, the farmer, consulting his own advantage, fought not against privilege or discrimination but against privileges for those who were not farmers.

The central emphasis of agrarian politics as the century began was on creating public instrumentalities to monitor the growth and the practices of the great consolidators. If most farmers stopped short of rural socialism, they also perpetuated the agrarian antimonopoly tradition. They would divide industrial power by enforcing the languishing antitrust law. They would bring industrial units down to their size. They would legislate their view of America as a middle-class society of independent husbandmen.

The laboring force, also troubled about the appurtenances of industrialism, was divided about how it wanted to employ the state. Crafts union leadership, representing skilled workers and by no means the majority of them, recognized the advantages to labor in the stability which restrictions of competition had achieved. The American Federation of Labor had no argument with the process of industrial consolidations, but it resented the application of antitrust laws to unions and their activities, and it demanded that the state protect the consolidations of workers that paralleled the consolidation of management. So protected, labor expected to obtain concessions in wages, hours and working conditions that would permit the workingman to increase his portion from industrial productivity and to live a decent life. For the same purpose, the crafts unions advocated legislation to set minimum standards of safety and sanitation and to insure an equitable system of workmen's compensation. The skilled laborer intended the state to promote his aspiration to the apparent status of the middle class.

The unskilled and unorganized, especially the recent immigrants, neither identified fully with the white-collar values of their blue-collar fellows nor stood to profit from the collective bargaining of the crafts. But the unskilled had hopes of their own which urban political machines were stimulating, as were the second-generation Americans who rooted their political careers in the advocacy of factory and tenement legislation, public health measures, and various forms of social insurance. For the laboring force, immigrant and native-born, they helped to create expectations of a society wherein the state underwrote minimum standards of life consonant with those that beguiled the trade unionist. Those standards implied a fair share in the nation's abundance and a full share of the minimum ingredients essential to self-esteem.

For such an urban and interdependent society, farmers ordinarily felt little sympathy; toward such an actionist and costly state, industrialists ordinarily felt only fear. Among laborer, farmer and industrialist, between any two of them, there was no sufficiently common identification of interest, no sufficiently common sense of purpose to effect a lasting collaboration.

☆

Politics, however, depended upon coalition, and the most effective one when the century began was the cooperation of business with urban political leadership. The extravagant behavior of that alliance and the conditions of filth and misery which it permitted to flourish offended the gentle ideals of many middle-class Americans, some of whom also resented the recruitment of a political elite from among the newly rich or the recently naturalized. But above all they were genuinely and righteously averse to dishonesty, to corruption blatantly paraded. The shame of the cities made itself felt first in the hearts of ladies and gentlemen of goodwill, of whom large numbers became reformers.

Some of the sturdiest and most conscientious dedicated themselves to social work, hoping thereby systematically to provide the services which urban politics rendered at best incompletely and unmethodically. As the social worker became familiar with his territory, however, he gradually recognized the need for political participation, for only by mobilizing the state could he hope to achieve precisely the ends for which the politically active second-generation Americans were also striving. From the ranks of the social workers there came a small but knowledgeable leadership for political reform and a trained and growing staff available to the state at any time it embarked upon remedial programs.

More immediately the reformer found himself in politics because of his attachment to good government. During the last decades of the nineteenth century scores of middle-class Americans devoted militant enthusiasm to civil service reform. As the century turned, these men were selecting new objectives designed to limit the power of the alliance of business with machine politics. They had discovered, moreover, that they could make their mark only by organizing, by consolidating their political activities just as the major political parties consolidated theirs. Ordinarily reform organizations had been nonpartisan, but they had therefore been ineffective, capable only of infrequent and inconclusive victories. Consequently the middle-class idealist moved more and more into the mainstream of politics itself. Accepting the terms of the two-party system, he tended by 1900 to work within one of the parties, suffering his defeats when they occurred without bolting, learning the necessity of gradualism and compromise.

Those who chose that avenue could pursue not only their ideals but also the satisfactions of high public office. What was more, they were able by judicious political regularity to enlist the allegiance of other groups, and they were forced, whatever preconceptions they brought to their role, to educate themselves in the needs and the methods of the rich, of the

poor, and of the rural. They were forced therefore to redis-
cover the gaps between the nation's actual achievements and
its various best hopes.

The politically active middle-class reformer became a kind
of self-appointed court to judge the processes and the possibilities of American politics. As he selected among the available
options, he tended, like representatives of other groups, to
identify with those to which he was drawn by his own experience and needs.

The eminent practicality of the middle-class political response revealed itself variously. Almost as much as the farmers, the managers of small business concerns suffered from the
latitude large industry enjoyed. With increasing frequency
they urged the use of the Sherman Antitrust Act to restore
equitable competition, the construction of public regulatory
agencies to discipline industrial power, and the increase of
funds available for business loans at moderate rates. The
spokesman of the urban middle class could go along with his
rural brother so long as the farmer did not insist on socialism
or upon federal adventures for which the city man had to pay.

Like the farmers and crafts union leaders, the middle-class
reformer worried about the unfamiliar way of life of the urban
masses. Through an easy rupture in logic he frequently
blamed the immigrant for the slums and sought remedy not
only in factory and tenement legislation, but also in the restriction of immigration. The industrial or residential slum,
furthermore, threatened property values which the owners of
better urban real estate were prepared to protect even at the
risk of some public expense. The social reformer, his self-
interest reinforcing his humanitarian zeal, asserted the desirability of raising the necessary public moneys by increasing

taxes on corporations and corporate properties. Such taxation could also support and improve public education, so long an issue of urgency for men who cherished high ambitions for their children. And graduated inheritance taxes were an attractive device for men determined to reduce the fortunes and the influence of the newly rich. Even the progressive income tax, once an amendment to the Constitution made it possible, constituted a larger threat to the owners of the great consolidations than to those who staffed their bureaucracies or managed their smaller competitors.

Prepared on their own account to question the status quo, middle-class social workers and political reformers took positions on public policy only marginally at variance with those of the moderates among farm and labor leaders. They took these positions, moreover, with a soothing conviction, in some cases justifiable and in all cases plausible, that they acted unselfishly for humanitarian goals. The middle-class man, alienated by extremes of wealth and poverty, frightened by the prospect of conflict between managers and laborers or urbanites and farmers that might disrupt the comfortable order of his society, sought out instinctively the conciliation that best suited the needs of effectual politics. He was admirably placed to be the competent broker of conflicting interests, to fashion a political purpose to which men from every sector of society might subscribe.

His conciliatory objective conformed exactly with the needs of the two major parties. In order to win a national election, to control not only the Presidency but also the houses of Congress, the major parties had to draw support from a complex of interest groups. Party success hinged on the ability of party leaders to control a shifting alignment of forces. To that end they could rely upon partisan loyalties to help cement coalitions, but these loyalties needed continually to be refreshed by techniques of reward and exhortation. The mobilization of political conviction depended in large part upon the availability of a national leader whose personality evoked sufficient attachment to convince those who suffered some disappointment in the process of compromise to follow where the party led. Through their leaders, through their platforms — loaded with the platitudes of a managed consensus — the national parties had to project an evocative program designed to obscure the concessions made by each element in any coalition large enough to govern, a program convincingly communicative of some promise for everyone.

The perfect source for such conciliation lay in the happy coincidence of middle-class values and political needs. A series of intraparty coalitions, each composed of different alignments of interest groups, successively dominated American politics during the first half of the twentieth century. Each depended upon middle-class support and middle-class leadership. The impellents of middle-class attitudes and the exigencies of coalition politics alike provoked a continual turning of the energies of the state toward a gradual reduction of the antitheses that characterized American life in 1900, and therefore toward a gradual fulfillment of the promises of the nation's heritage. In this process, both the accomplishments and the rhetoric of the successful coalitions revealed the essentially constant, preponderantly middle-class aspirations which Americans expected their politics to effectuate. And as in earlier years, successful American political leaders symbolized the range of national ideals and the changing priorities among them.

☆

Theodore Roosevelt, inheriting the presidency in 1901, set out to capture the allegiance of "the farmers, small businessmen and upper-class mechanics" whom he considered his "natural allies." They had been, he felt, the natural allies of Lincoln, in Roosevelt's view the greatest President and the best American. Patrician though he was, Roosevelt had a genius for reaching the average voters, for endowing his deliberately commonplace statements of middle-class virtues with the drama of his own exuberance. For all the superficial differences between himself and his electorate, he contended, down at bottom they had the same ideals.

Roosevelt presided over a centrist coalition. Though it included moderates from agriculture and labor, it rested upon the sure foundation of the Republican precincts, strongest in the East and Middle West, and it attracted, as the party so long had, most men of wealth who in any case had no ready political alternative. Roosevelt assiduously cultivated his organization, rewarding regularity without condoning corruption, binding the professionals and their constituents to his person. The special needs of politics motivated his solicitous gestures toward populous religious and ethnic groups, Catholics, Jews and Methodists; Germans, Hungarians, Irishmen, Italians and Bohemian-Americans; and Negroes, too, whose candidates for preferment were selected for the President by Booker T. Washington.

Quite apart from politics, Roosevelt felt a special responsibility for his entire constituency. "My view," he wrote, "was that every executive officer, and above all every executive officer in high position, was a steward of the people bound actively and affirmatively to do all he could for the people." He summoned to executive office and as consultants to its incumbents those "best minds" — the captains of industry, law and finance — in whose allegiance the Republicans took such pride. Beyond that, he invited to the White House interpreters of the whole range of American culture, poets and writers, inventors and explorers, economists and sociologists, professors and ministers of the gospel, to all of whom he listened and to all of whom he preached. His style especially impressed young men who responded to his call for disinterested national duty. Never in any country had Lord Bryce, discerning critic of things American, seen a more eager, high-spirited or efficient set of public servants. They cleansed Washington of the Midas mood of earlier years; they provided the expert advice on which the President so methodically relied. The political and administrative structure of Roosevelt's government mirrored his private, reflective temperament which he so often dressed in an adventurous vocabulary.

Roosevelt's Square Deal gave a circumspect, urban, paternalistic direction to change. His most winning gestures toward the farmer were those that had an equal appeal to small business. The first President to employ the Sherman Antitrust Law aggressively, he established the usefulness of that act for dissolving industrial combinations. But he placed his larger faith in regulation. Antitrust he considered important as a kind of sheep dog, perpetually barking at the flock to keep it in order but rarely allowed to snap except at a stubborn stray. Industrialism, he believed, required consolidation. For society to live with consolidation, however, government had to have the power to monitor the behavior of big business, and government had also to encourage farm and labor organizations which, once constructed, would tend to balance the power of industry. His emphasis was on balance rather than destruction, on countervalence rather than fragmentation.

This protected — even endorsed — the economic structure of American industrialism without endorsing — indeed while limiting — the license of industrial power.

Roosevelt's policies underwrote all the pleasing conditions of modern industrial civilization, the conveniences, the productivity, the national strength which only the nostalgic wished to remove from American life. He nourished the national dream of plenty. Yet his rhetoric tempered the acceptance of bigness with a more popular invocation of moral individuality and absolute justice. Condemning only the criminal and foolish among the rich, the violent and sullen among the poor, the corrupt and timid without regard to income, Roosevelt welcomed all others as his partners in a program of "common sense, courage and common honesty." They believed him, by and large, as they should have, for he was himself the heroic image of his constituency.

On two accounts the centrist coalition fell apart after Roosevelt left office. His successor, William Howard Taft, a genial man without nerve for politics, let himself be identified with, if not captured by, the right wing of his party. Roosevelt had struck many poses — cowboy, soldier, explorer, policeman — familiar and endearing to the American people. But as he observed in 1908, Taft risked disfavor by having his photograph so often taken while he played golf, then still a rich man's game. So also, though Taft judged public policy much as Roosevelt would have, he seemed to lack vigor, imagination, and especially the common touch. Almost before he was at home in the White House, the young stewards of the Roosevelt years were leaving government, and the spokesmen of agricultural discontent and middle-class reform were drifting away from the Republicans. Taft's maladroitness was not alone to blame. Industrial interests and their advocates had decided they preferred control of the party to government of the country. As the fringes of the coalition raveled, the party came to represent primarily the more privileged Americans.

This gave the Democrats a splendid opportunity to form a broad coalition of their own. What evolved in the years between 1910 and 1916 was a new reformist coalition rather more rural than its predecessor. It contained the solid South, largely agricultural, and the dependable urban Democratic machines, but it grew beyond that bifurcated base to take in many of those whom Taft's associates had alienated. Building on the foundations Roosevelt's Republicans had laid, modifying but not abandoning their picture of society, Wilson's Democracy made large alterations in the pattern of American life.

Perhaps no American ever surpassed Woodrow Wilson's talent for expressing Christian hope. That gift was the product of a soul imbued with the best of a Presbyterian ethic, of a spirit in harmony with the faith of Emerson, of a mind taught to perceive the possibilities of liberalism and to manage the rhetoric of persuasion, of a temperament saturated in certitude. Wilson was a Southerner proud alike of his section and his nation, an educator dedicated to training for government an elite of talent, and an American historian captivated by the virtues of Washington and Lincoln. His qualities of person and their projection in his elegant speech excited for a bright season the idealism of the middle class.

By his own account a spokesman of the aspirant small businessman, of the "man on the make," by temperament and training suspicious of organized power, Wilson put his first emphasis on measures designed "to cleanse, to reconsider, to restore." The initial statutory achievements of his New Freedom tended to curb industrial power. They also gave the country for the first time a central banking system susceptible to considerable public control. Further, Wilson brought back to federal administration much of the excellence that had departed with Roosevelt. Those innovations satisfied Wilson's modest reformist proclivities, but in order to enlarge his coalition he espoused a number of measures he had previously resisted, including legislation establishing the eight-hour day on railroads, creating special federal banks to make inexpensive loans to farmers, and prohibiting child labor. After the coming of war, he accepted without complaint the heavy, deliberately redistributive taxes imposed by Congress.

Yet Wilson's management of his party gave small satisfaction to unorganized workers, the majority of the laboring force. Only with unfeigned reluctance did the President cooperate with the leaders of the Democracy of the cities to whom he gave no feeling of belonging. In some areas of the country he withheld the favors to which machine Democrats had long been accustomed. He had no clearly communicable argument with nativism or with Prohibition, the anathemas of city wards. To the damage of his party in northern areas to which Negroes were migrating in increasing volume, he allowed segregation of federal facilities in Washington for the first time since the Civil War. Especially in the East, the Democratic urban vote showed some tendency to waver when it came to electing national officials.

Wilson always appealed more to the America of the small town and polite suburb than to the America of the blast furnace and asphalt pavement. His prim middle-classness, dressed in an antiseptic rectitude, had political force just so long as he bent to agrarian demands and engaged himself in completing his generation's program of middle-class reform, of what seemed, at least, to be the insulation of politics from the rule of the machines and of industrial power from the domination of wealth. Thereafter the middle-class man began to feel he had conceded enough to the less privileged, and Wilson's interpretation of the mission of America as an exemplary, moral force suited his constituency only while the strains of war invigorated his plea for mutual sacrifice. Even then there were grumblings from industrialists yearning for freedom from federal control, from farmers chafing at ceilings on the price of wheat, from ethnic groups unpersuaded by the President's implicit Anglo-Saxonism, and from erstwhile reformers saturated with change and tired of high taxes. Whatever its merit, the apocalyptical image Wilson offered to them neither satisfied their particular interests nor provided the political beguilement of Roosevelt's sometimes banal but always vigorous practicality.

☆

The disruption of the Democratic coalition coincided with the obdurate self-seeking of its separate parts. Satisfied with what government had accomplished, the middle-class man reidentified with wealth or the exciting prospect of wealth and reenlisted with the Republicans. The urban machines reestablished their immunity from genteel intrusions and reasserted their antipathy to agrarian culture. Throughout the 1920's the most obvious characteristic of the Democratic Party was its incoherence. Lacking a purpose that could obscure the incompatibility of the rural South and the urban North, lacking a middle-class leadership that could fuse the two, the party could barely nominate and could not elect a Presidential candidate. It could find no conciliatory formula for itself, much less a program for the nation.

Men of wealth and their standpat representatives who had chosen to control the Republican Party even at the risk of its defeat collected their reward after 1918. Content to let the Democratic factions neutralize each other, they systematically nullified the effect of most of the reform legislation of the previous two decades by turning government over to ineffectual administrators, by reducing the income tax, by re-enthroning industry and its privileges. This regression to conditions as they had been was possible only because of the changes that had occurred. Though the bastions of reform had become paper fortresses, the tired progressive was content with the semblance of success. He had no stomach either for subsidizing agriculture or for effecting a broad redistribution of income and property. He was happily seduced by the prosperity of the golden twenties. The cornucopia of advancing industrialism overflowed to the unprecedented benefit not of its masters alone but also of their bureaucratic, legal, medical and aesthetic servants. Industry took care, too, to allot some of the increase in productivity to labor. Business paternalism for the time made the doctrines of a magnanimous stewardship amply satisfying. The organized labor movement receded, losing both membership and spirit, smug in the false comfort it drew from the restriction of immigration which it helped to effect.

Calvin Coolidge's laconic complacency mirrored the temper of the time. Measured in terms of his capacity to represent a total constituency, Coolidge was a superlative President. He was "sincerely, genuinely, terribly crazy" about wealth. Though his hobby, he once said, was "holdin' office," he was devoted to laissez-faire government. "Four-fifths of all our troubles would disappear," he believed, "if we would only sit down and do nothing." He stood as plausibly as Wilson had for middle-class rectitude and much more obviously than his immediate precessors for petty bourgeois caution. A more skillful politician than Wilson, indeed in his operations within the party as self-aggrandizing as Roosevelt, Coolidge also had a sure instinct for speaking the transient mind of his people. His was the appropriate symbolism of his decade, for it believed with him that the man who built a factory built a temple, and the man who worked there worshiped there. While this spirit reigned, only the fact of prosperity remained to level further the still blatant antitheses of the society.

Both the political strength of the administration and the persuasion of its message depended upon prosperity. It was prosperity that perpetuated the cleavages that separated Yankee from immigrant workers and both from farmers. It was prosperity that gave an aura of reality to the incantations that beclouded the retreat of the state. But prosperity was transitory. Indeed the failure of government even to attempt to close the gap between the rich and the poor safeguarded a maldistribution of income which contributed to economic collapse after 1929. In the next years the vicissitudes of depression reemphasized the polarity in American life.

Much of the middle class, its savings and security threatened, lost confidence in Republican stewardship. The paternalism of industry disappeared with the decline of profits, and with an awful aloneness laborers met the misery of unemployment which neither the tired clichés of union leadership nor the overtaxed resources of urban politicians could mitigate. The farmer, the victim of an agricultural slump that antedated the crash itself, harassed by falling income and heavy debts, faced the harrowing loss of independence and self-respect. Among the captains of industry and finance, too, especially among those whose profits had disappeared and whose businesses seemed about to, there was a growing sentiment for mobilizing the state in self-protection. The folklore of Coolidge could not meet the needs of any group. The "best minds," including Herbert Hoover's, too often counseled only patience and prudence, qualities vastly unconvincing in the absence of prosperity.

☆

By 1932 the Democratic Party could scarcely have failed to achieve power. Under the astute leadership of Franklin Roosevelt, it also achieved triumph. Again and again he modeled his career and policies on those of his "Uncle Ted" who was, he often said, the greatest man he ever knew. But the second Roosevelt was more democratic in spirit as well as in party than the first, more sympathetic to the distinctive tonalities of Jefferson and Jackson, and of Wilson and Bryan, too. "Plenty is at our doorstep," Franklin Roosevelt told the nation when he assumed office, in a phrase that recalled agrarian oratory of the depression of forty years before, "but a generous use of it languishes in the very sight of the supply. Primarily this is because rules of the exchange of mankind's goods have failed . . . Practices of the unscrupulous money changers stand indicted in the court of public opinion." Those money changers, he continued, with the venom Theodore Roosevelt had reserved for "malefactors of great wealth," had fled "from their high seats in the temple of civilization. We may now restore that temple to the ancient truths."

The symbol of that restoration and of the national purpose it renewed, Roosevelt recaptured the spirit and refurbished the rhetoric of reform. His New Deal rested in uneasy equilibrium, as he so often put it, somewhere slightly left of center, but the coalition over which he presided delivered something to the disenchanted in every sector of society. In the period 1932 through 1938 it conceded less and less to the business community and more and more to agriculture and labor. Yet those concessions were continuously modified by the basic commitment of the New Deal to the enduring American heritage and its middle-class values.

Like his namesake in office, Franklin Roosevelt accepted the condition of size in industry as a fact of life. In spite of delayed and unconvincing antitrust activity, the New Deal endeavored to contain the power of industry rather than to pulverize it. It increased the number and the authority of federal regulative agencies. It transferred the determining voice in monetary and banking policy to the government. It put government into the business of regional development, a business private capital could not and would not sustain. It made government big, and yet it left business as big as ever and potentially much bigger. Size, to which few Americans really objected, was newly dignified, for besides big government, the New Deal sponsored big labor and big agriculture, thereby achieving that balance of social forces which the Square Deal had anticipated. There was a kind of leveling up of the consolidations of American life that the rhetoric of the day accurately equated with a leveling down of privilege.

The balances thereby established left the small entrepreneur, the professional man, the pensioner, without the strength to resist the organized interests which were capable of making agreements between themselves that might threaten those who lived outside of their orbits. But for the persisting commitment of the society to bourgeois and individualistic values, the New Deal wrote special insurance. As it did to industry, it supplied to farmers and homeowners generous and cheap credit to protect mortgaged properties which might otherwise have been foreclosed and to assist in the acquisition of new and better farms and homes. The state in effect wrote for itself a money license to guard small and large capitalists, householders, self-employed farmers and those who desired to become self-employed, from the perils of the business cycle. In using this license, moreover, the government strengthened private lending institutions by employing public credit indirectly, by insuring private sources of capital against much of the risk of lending.

While underwriting the security of private property, the New Deal expanded the benefactions, the attractiveness, and the authority of federal government. Early agricultural legislation guaranteed many farmers a decent subsistence, and later, when the level of parity was redefined during the Second World War, an outright prosperity. So also with labor. The government set minimum standards for wages and hours, adopted national programs for unemployment and old age insurance, and began, if only haltingly, to replace slums with public housing projects. Further, New Deal politics cultivated the matured ambitions of American minorities. Republican government during the 1920's had been predominately Protestant and Lily White. Democratic government in the next decade welcomed to federal office the talent and influence of vigorous young descendants, born American, of Irish and Jewish, Italian and Polish immigrants. So, too, Democrats in the

North assisted the impoverished Negro, though not equally with the impoverished white, and opportunely found prestigious posts for cooperative Negro leaders. Even the federal bench, long a sanctuary of ethnic privilege, was opened more widely to the appointments of judges recruited from a multiethnic bar.

Indeed the Supreme Court itself yielded to the forces of change. The restrictive doctrine of substantive due process and the restrictive interpretation of federal power to control commerce that had hampered government since the 1890's provided the bases for the Court's nullifications of much early New Deal legislation, but after 1937, prodded by Roosevelt's attacks and altered by his appointments, the Supreme Court at late last abandoned the jurisprudence of the industrialists.

All in all, New Deal policies tended to level the status of the separate groups in the United States toward a mean which seemed golden to all but the wealthy. The prescriptions and the success of federally supported collective bargaining opened labor unions to the unskilled and brought within them a significant fraction of the working force, while the bargaining process itself helped them to extract from industry a growing share of the proceeds of production. Federal spending for relief and work relief not only saved a fifth of the nation from destitution but also established the obligation of the state to defend the right to work, and to work at something above subsistence pay. Perhaps more significantly, the New Dealers, building on earlier precedents, made of the personal and corporate income taxes and the personal estate and gift taxes, potent egalitarian instruments. The acquisition and transmission of great fortunes became extremely difficult except in a few fields of activity which special interest groups contrived to protect. Against the tax laws more than any other New Deal venture, men of wealth protested.

Roosevelt delighted in announcing he planned it that way, delighted in flagellating the rich by ridiculing what "they say" in mellifluous and colloquial addresses to the total people, "my friends." As he said, they were his friends. That Rooseveltian smile, that broad Rooseveltian "hello" which Winston Churchill somewhere called the most wonderful word in the English language, those white shirt-sleeves waving from an open Ford, those hot dogs that the President made the special fare of royalty, all these and more made Roosevelt the good neighbor of every man next door in town, and of every man who learned from Roosevelt to believe that he could and should and would soon move next door. The squire of the Hudson was the winning tribune of the American plebian. There was in the New Deal a joy and a promise that mitigated the impact of continuing hard times. There was, too, in the New Deal an element of the carnival on Saturday night, an element of the cocky and the gaudy, a kind of bravado, that dispelled the moralism and the paternalism of earlier episodes in humanitarian striving. A vulgarizing of middle-class reform as well as a broadening of its mission gave it a larger and more dedicated constituency who not only profited from its works but also reveled in its showmanship.

☆

New Deal efforts at reform proved more successful than New Deal efforts at recovery. The intensification of depression in 1937 and 1938 drove marginal voters from the Democratic coalition. So, too, did the leveling up that occasioned a growing resentment among those comfortable men who pre-

ferred their stations to carry an element of exclusiveness. En-
listing with the more elite, they formed a sufficiently strong
veto group, partly within and partly without the Democratic
Party, to block the attempts of agriculture and laboring interests further to help themselves. But with prosperity's return
during the Second World War, the devices for leveling and
for counterbalancing which the New Deal had created held
the allegiance of all but a small minority of the people. In a
time of plenty the institutional pressures militating toward an
egalitarian distribution of the products of the economy operated so dramatically that most Americans felt themselves becoming members of the middle class.

In the years after the war wages and hours legislation and
expansions of federal social insurance scarcely kept pace with
the rising wages of the laboring force; returns from federal taxation increased relatively less than did disposable consumer income. Few of the terrors of early-century agricultural distress
remained. The farmer, if he suffered at all, suffered only by
comparison with the servants of industrialism. The great consolidations emerged from the New Deal and the war stronger
and better respected than ever before. Though their power
over labor was partially checked by the power of the unions,
in spite of a decline in union membership, and though their
power over their competitors was subject to continual but
bland sniping by antitrust and federal regulation, they confronted no debilitating obstacles to their pursuit of markets
and of profits.

Most important, the upward march of the agricultural and
laboring force left older members of the middle class, and a
legion of new recruits to management and clerical employment, in a position relatively less privileged than it had been

fifty or even twenty years earlier. The small businessman, professional man or bureaucrat became more concerned with protecting himself than with assisting the unfortunate. Though some 10 per cent of all Americans remained impoverished or at least uncomfortable, the middle class by and large had lost most of its altruistic consciousness of positive political mission.

Because the antitheses of the early twentieth century diminished, so also did demand for further evolution of the energies of the state. The various interest groups were committed less to change than to the preservation of their gains, and therefore to the status quo. Under those conditions the conciliatory processes of politics rested close to dead center. That was the source and meaning of "moderation" — the state of mind which elected federal governments that could not rule, governments in which neither party commanded a working alliance, governments without a mandate.

Harry S Truman stood with spirited impatience against the encroaching complacency of his countrymen and their representative congresses. In political life perhaps the most genuine example of national possibilities and individual self-improvement since Lincoln, Truman at his frequent bravest surpassed the sentiments of his background, but the biases of stealthy respectability he never wholly purged. His Fair Deal attempted to drive forward the kinds of programs that had faltered since 1938. He cared, as those with conscience in the middle class still cared, about the failures of the mission of America, about the plights of the indigent ignorant, the sick and lonely aged, the abandoned children of fractured homes, the Negroes especially, victims of the prejudice and segregation that the President's Commission on Civil Rights so lucidly denounced. But in domestic matters Truman was rarely a successful chief executive, and he was never a generally beloved President. The spunky purpose and prickly dignity that captured the affection and fidelity of his ablest intimates grated against the smug torpor of the times.

The appropriate symbol for the conditions and the mood of "moderation" was displayed not in Truman but in Dwight David Eisenhower. A middle-aged, middle-class man who gave almost all of his active life to expert service for the federal government, General Eisenhower cared about the good of all Americans but trusted the more privileged, by and large, to prescribe for themselves and for all others. Like so many among the millions of his middle-class admirers, he was a kindly but a rather tired man. Conciliation, as Ike practiced it in politics, proposed an end to conflicts of interests not through the energy of resolution but through the stolidity of forbearance. As he wished, he found himself, to a degree unprecedented in the history of American politics, the symbol, serene and unassailable, of both parties.

Yet the ancient truths were not bereft of youth and vigor. Just as the election of John Fitzgerald Kennedy signaled the full acceptance by the nation of the Catholic Irish, whose calculating, even arrogant herald fitted the model for national responsibility cast by Theodore Roosevelt six decades earlier, so did Kennedy himself direct the force of federal government to assist the kinds of groups whose lot had contradicted the promise of America before and in and after Franklin Roosevelt's tenure. The motion that the New Frontier imparted to the country was toward fulfillment of the very goals inherent in an heroic reading of the destiny of the United States. It was not immediately an adequate thrust, but its courageous and sufficient promise explained the guilt and grief and reawakened purpose that flowed from Kennedy's sudden, violent, horrid death.

The large task remaining, his successor said, was the task defined by Lincoln's dreams. That task, he added, would remain so long as there was "a child without a school . . . a man without a job, a family without a home," so long as there were "sick Americans without medical care or aging Americans without hope" or "any Americans, of any race . . . denied their full human rights." To the hope that Lyndon Johnson expressed — the hope, he said, of a prudent progressive — Americans had long subscribed. Toward its realization the continual accommodations of middle-class politics had worked for over sixty years. The great men of the distant past had had their heirs; the culture in its best seasons had preserved their vision — still beckoning, still exemplary — of a bountiful society in which each man had assurance of comfort and of dignity and of freedom in all just pursuits.

Chapter

5

☆ ☆ ☆ ☆ ☆

THE ULTIMATE

MORALITY

WHILE THE PROCESSES of politics operated to make concrete the aspirations of the middle class, those aspirations, like that class itself, were changing. Most just pursuits in 1900 remained associated, as they had been for a century and more, with work — with striving, with occupations, with their rewards. During the following fifty years, however, in the culture of an advancing technology and an expanding economy, Americans had also increasingly to concern themselves with leisure, its uses and allocation. Leisure promised its own satisfactions, but Americans knew few precedents for evaluating them. They had been too busy, too involved in conquering the continent and developing and distributing its resources, to give leisure the attention it required. Leisure had ordinarily been deemed a luxury, sometimes even a corrupt one, for leisure, when the century turned, had yet properly to be differentiated from indolence and ostentation, which the culture spurned.

The national hero of 1903, Theodore Roosevelt, told one audience that work was "absolutely necessary . . . no man can be said to live in the true sense of the word, if he does not work." Roosevelt conceived of work exactly as Benjamin Franklin had. Industry and frugality, essential virtues for social progress, were also the required qualities for riches, success and social status. Time saved from work belonged to self-improvement, national duty, service to nature or mankind. Idleness, like extravagance, was a folly of the immoral; rest, like food, a fuel to be consumed when work began again. In that vein Thorstein Veblen made the leisure class the target of his censures, and reserved his fondest blessings for the "engineers," creatively productive men whose fulfillment came from work.

Little though they seemed to understand it, Roosevelt and Veblen were members of a generation that lived through the stage of mechanization which carried the United States once and for all across the brink of industrial abundance. The twentieth century was still young when Henry Ford and Frederick Winslow Taylor, devoted disciples of the gospel of work, accomplished their prodigies of production, when during the First World War the United States supplied not only its own ordinary and emergency needs but also the extraordinary demands of western Europe. Certainly by 1915, probably years earlier, the nation had in hand the resources and the techniques to furnish luxuries as well as necessities for a far larger population than it contained. The engineers, when Veblen arranged their apotheosis, had already worked their powerful magic on the price system, and the strenuous life, when Roosevelt lived it, had to spend its furious energies seeking adventures as substitutes for useful work.

By that time the cult of work, thrift and success had lost some of its following. Labor was persuaded that the earth would spin just as swiftly if the workday were nearer eight hours than ten. The owners of the machines that helped to encourage that persuasion still resisted it, often with the argument that hard work never hurt anybody, but some of them were also in their own ways violating the cult. Their vacations had become longer, many of their children were devoted to play, and their frugality had often surrendered to the purchase of expensive playthings. They were adumbrating, as it were, a cult of consumption, whereas those who in their youth had convenanted with the gospel of work clung to their conflicting ethic. The conflict tested middle-class values, whose continuing integrity depended on a reconciliation, yet to be achieved, of affluence with virtue and of leisure with freedom.

☆

So strong was the national faith in work that it instructed later generations. Some twenty years after Roosevelt's most successful campaign, Calvin Coolidge still spoke in a metaphor that interchanged factories and cathedrals. One bestselling author of the 1920's, not content with the imagery of the national past, discovered that Christ had been a businessman. "Jesus," he preached, ". . . picked up twelve men from the bottom ranks of business and forged them into an organization that conquered the world . . . Great progress will be made . . . when we rid ourselves of the idea that there is a difference between *work* and *religious work*." Devoutly in agreement, the chairman of the board of a large corporation employed Horatio Alger's language to explain the promotion of a company officer. "I'd put it this way," he said, "Albert Salt was the best office boy we ever had, the best clerk we ever had, the best salesman we ever had, the best purchasing agent we ever had, and he never knew when the whistle blew."

Such homilies still titillated the middle class. Popular novels and stories, repeating the success parable, held up to Albert Salt and his would-be companions a glass in which they could admire themselves. The same novels suggested that idleness and elegance alike encouraged licentiousness, a disease to which artists and intellectuals, presumably marginal workers at best, were particularly subject. Greenwich Village and the Left Bank were havens of exiles, as one of them recalled, who were fleeing the culture of their high schools, the still virulent cult of work. Even Franklin during the 1920's was rather less popular as a symbol than was Albert Salt, for unlike him, Franklin had a cultivated taste for wine and women, rest and speculation — diversions from productive work and careful thrift that undid Sinclair Lewis's Sam Dodsworth.

As middle-class readers pitied him, so did they honor Herbert Hoover who, it seemed, had walked right out of American mythology. Son of an Iowa farmer, orphaned at ten, Hoover had gone west, worked his way through Stanford University, battled the fraternities there, married a banker's daughter, and earned his first million dollars before he was forty. He dispensed food to the starving Belgians during the Great War and managed American relief in Europe after it, establishing a reputation equally for efficiency and humanitarianism. Though an English associate, stunned by the price Hoover demanded for American pork, judged privately that he counted hogs in his sleep, farmers in the corn belt, had they known, would have celebrated that practice, too. Back in the United States, Hoover as Secretary of Commerce promoted trade and investment abroad, befriended industrial associations, fought waste in government, and expected business, with the help of his department and of God, to banish poverty from the land. An Albert Salt on an Olympian scale, Hoover until 1929 was esteemed as the most virtuous of all American engineers.

Esteem was the ultimate article of the total faith in work, but the neat progression from work and thrift to riches and social status faced a powerful challenge during the 1920's. Americans were then shown a shortcut to esteem — a shortcut that reckoned thrift a vice. With the problem of production solved industry's next problem was sales, and its next solution, advertising, which had to reach and stimulate the national market. In order to teach Americans to buy more than they needed, though rarely as much as their growing enterprises were producing, advertising had to disseminate an abbreviated image of the good life. It sold esteem.

Of course it also sold many other good things. Advertisements for soap sold cleanliness; for orange juice, health; for mouth wash, romantic love. But most of all advertising sold success. These clothes, that furniture, this house, and especially those automobiles signified success. Ownership brought success itself, ordinarily in company with a beautiful woman, and ownership was simplified. One could buy today and pay tomorrow in regular, small instalments. No need to wait, no need to save, and the interest rate, while hideous, was hidden.

As the advertising profession so often claimed, its techniques exposed demands rather than creating them. The exposure necessarily associated available and marketable commodities with more remote and sometimes impalpable aspirations. Powerful aspirations, after all, long predated the layouts that translated sex into antiperspirants and vigor into breakfast cereals. So, too, and emphatically, with status. If success had not already become an American fetish, advertising could scarcely have invented it. The triumph of advertising derived from divorcing esteem from sweat and self-denial.

Similarly advertising encouraged waste. Alfred Sloan understood the situation exactly. Mechanization, he realized, permitted General Motors to manufacture cars much faster than its customers could use them up. As one executive put it, "the old factors of wear and tear can no longer be depended upon to create a demand." Neither could beauty or performance alone, but advertising could hasten obsolescence, and though some company engineers were unhappy, G.M. made fashion the pavement of its road to glory. As with automobiles, so with many consumer items, the date and packaging determined the measure of esteem.

Yet here again advertising was rather more revealing than revolutionary. Waste had always attended American experience in abundance. The nation had condoned a profligate use of land and minerals and reckless spoilage of timber, water, even air. But if waste had long existed, it had not been counted a quality of success. Rascals were spendthrift, but good men, wise and frugal, until advertising drew a beard on savers and shaved clean the purchasers of fashion.

In attaching esteem to ownership, as it did, advertising substituted a static value for the kinetic attributes of the Alger story. The fact of acquisition replaced the process of achievement. The success image lost its motion. That was a portentous but possibly essential change, for the kind of work available to most Americans, including those of the middle class, was becoming increasingly lusterless. By redefining the image, the hucksters distorted it, to be sure, but they also preserved it. The Alger story was, among other things, one expression of a larger vision of a society of opportunity, plenty, and human dignity. Madison Avenue, contriving a new recipe from old ingredients, simply associated opportunity and dignity with shared abundance. That association emphasized the standard of living instead of the nature of work as the gauge of esteem, especially of self-esteem. With high wages, a laborer, however mean his job, could be fashionable, and therefore, in his view and that of many others, successful.

Advertising also contributed to the corruption of earlier ideas about work. Artificial obsolescence was a continuing charge against the integrity of a product and consequently against the satisfactions of manufacturing it. There could be small sense of purpose in making something only to have it sold and then soon thrown away. Doubtless mechanization itself cost laborers much of their involvement in their jobs and perhaps all of their identification with their products. Advertising, by encouraging waste, at the very least exaggerated the resulting loss of dignity in work. Albert Salt never knew when the whistle blew, but he was an office worker and executive. His counterpart at a punching machine, who "didn't drink . . . or read or think," was employed in a routinized job fabricating a disposable artifact distinguished primarily by its salability. Hating his job, he heard the whistle loud and clear. So also did those clerical and professional workers whose own functions were made more and more mechanized, more and more specialized, more and more routine. The Algerine view of virtuous industry could not flourish where labor lacked mission and work lacked joy.

Perhaps just in time, the changing culture endorsed the ready compensations of more income and more leisure, luxuries that a bountiful technology made possible. Advertising did not destroy the old cult. Rather, it expressed the values of a society in which there were few real problems of production. The culprit, if there was a culprit, often used the name of progress. Yet the pressures of mechanization and advertising together hastened the denigration of industriousness and furthered the emulative consumption and conspicuous leisure that had so disquieted Veblen.

Advertising also created and sold reputations. Public relations experts, masters of the new art of ballyhoo, endowed insurance and utilities companies, as well as other corporations, with qualities of nobility previously unnoticed by their competitors and customers. Ballyhoo provided, too, engaging personalities for otherwise boorish stars of cinema and sport whose feats of love and muscle were peddled as spectaculars to a beholding public eager in their leisure to consume vicarious glory. Indeed the buncombe that built synthetic heroes inspired a misplaced cynicism, a debunking of the genuine rather than the sham. The carelessness of advertising, however inadvertent, magnified the confusion of American values it exposed.

☆

Those who had absorbed the dogma of consumption suffered special frustrations during the Great Depression, for the identification of fashion with esteem spelled failure when incomes and savings dwindled or disappeared. Madison Avenue, spokesman for the culture, had sold to broker and laborer alike automobiles and silk shirts as substitutes for the satisfactions of involvement. Now the broker had to abide last year's models, and the laborer, his job gone and his time-payments in arrears, had to surrender his insignia of success and his creature comforts, too. As they had before, moreover, the unemployed discovered that involuntary idleness, no kin to leisure, lacked the qualities of self-indulgent ease or self-selected play.

Nevertheless, the conditions of depression did not expunge archaic interpretations of the cult of work, to which business managers and their associates by and large adhered. A man, they still maintained, was worth the wages that he earned and so it followed that unemployment still arose from "thriftlessness, sin in various forms, disease." By those standards, the government erred doubly in providing jobs for the needy. First, in their disgrace, the unemployed deserved no help. Second, expenditures for work relief were offset in part by federal taxes that penalized accumulations of industry and frugality and thus punished virtue. Alternatively deficits defrayed the rising costs of government, but deficits, worse even than taxes, revealed the ultimate corruption of prodigality.

So construed, the ethic of the cult of work arraigned both social reform and economic reason. Federal old age and survivors insurance, and federal compensation for unemployment would "take away from mankind the impulse to save" and thus destroy "one of the fundamental elements of human character." Those programs would decrease "individual energy and efficiency," "take all the romance out of life," and open "pathways" to the "downfall of Rome." Most horrendous were the implications of deliberate countercyclical spending, whose opponents in the United States drew less inspiration from Ricardo than from Poor Richard. Though the Great Depression arose from too much saving, too little investment, during its long tenure, as indeed for years thereafter, the champions of balancing the budget in every circumstance cited by name "the Puritan ethic" and called on prudence to answer Keynes.

The rags-to-riches story, however, had lost its appeal for those Americans wearing rags, as well as for the many more whose expectations advertising had long nurtured. Most of the latter group accepted, or at least condoned, federal insurance of bank accounts and against destitution, federal subsidies for electricity and roads, federal aid for buying or improving homes. In a similar spirit, recipients of the federal veterans' bonus of 1936 quickly spent the proceeds from their bonds, often for new cars.

Recipients of the jobs the government created needed the satisfactions of employment as much as the goods and services they then could buy. Indeed the depression reminded Americans of the importance of work in itself as well as in its role as a measure of status or a means for acquisitiveness. Like their detractors, jobless men ascribed to themselves the guilt of inadequacy. A sense of failure, growing with each month of inactivity, left thousands of laborers hopeless, and demoralized the unemployed of the middle class who struggled to effect appearances they could no longer sustain. "The young," moreover, in the observation of one New Dealer, were "rotting without jobs." The dole, as Roosevelt said, was "a narcotic, a subtle destroyer of the human spirit." The able-bodied looking for employment, he believed, had a right to work, and the federal government advanced that right, within the limits of the possible, by placing men and women in positions designed to preserve their skills as well as their self-esteem. Emergency federal employment perforce dispensed mostly routine jobs, but the government utilized the talents of architects and engineers in designing the bridges and schools and dams it built, of teachers in programs of free instruction for adults, of lawyers and accountants in administering the operations of the others. Further, the Federal Writers Project gave work to authors and poets, the Federal Theater Project employed actors and directors, the Federal Art Project hired sculptors and painters, the National Youth Administration found part-time assignments for college students, often in exercises related to their studies. The right to work, as the New Deal finally understood it, included opportunity for the dignity and satisfaction of professional or artistic self-expression. The critics of the New Deal, those who fancied themselves the high priests of the cult of work, especially objected to the costs and principle of subsidizing programs that permitted personal fulfillment. Work, according to those critics, occurred only in the marketplace, which in their construction alone enjoyed the privilege of allocating the surpluses from production to art or other leisure callings.

Ironically the New Dealers could offer the unskilled no prospect more satisfying than reemployment in that marketplace. Experiments with self-help, with furnishing the unemployed with raw materials to convert to food and clothes and artifacts for communities set apart to be self-sufficient, mocked the realities of the industrialized society in which the jobless had their roots. The more common alternative, the manual tasks of work relief, required kinds of labor that aroused little zeal. Accordingly the meager wages of work relief limited those who earned them to meager satisfactions in consumption as well as on the job. The nearest escape lay in the higher pay of the private sector and the comforts and fashions that pay could purchase. In the private sector, too, many jobs were merely drudgery, a condition set by mechanization half a century before. Consequently in the 1930's, as in the previous and successive decades, most of the laboring force considered less physical work for more spendable pay an unmitigated gain.

The apparent agencies for that gain, rather than the oppressive jobs, evoked the workers' loyalties. On that account the labor unions received the grateful allegiance of their members, and the New Deal, protector of the unions, won the affection of its wards. Union locals operated, in one sense, as clubs whose members, true to each other and to their leaders, were united against their opponents, even other unions, and hostile or uncomprehending toward criticism, particularly toward censures derived from management's cult of work. Union officials, like precinct captains before them, took care of their following and of themselves, now and then with scant regard for means; in rare but troubling cases with small concern for law. When they were attacked, whether justly or not, their constituents felt embattled, apprehensive lest they lose their share in the general allocation of resources, their share of the substitutes for engagement and of the symbols of self-esteem.

That was precisely the attitude also of a host of men whose overalls had a tailored cut. They valued the income from their callings or the prestige of their professions. Their loyalty flowed to their companies, their providers of employment and companionship and favor, the lodges where they felt that they belonged. They were involved less in work than in the security of status. Regrettable though their lack of engagement was, it was not immoral, and during the depression especially, it was not attributable to abundance or to advertising. Success itself, after all, rather than the labor that produced it, beguiled the antagonists of reform, who also seemed to believe that the comfort they enjoyed would damage the character of those who had yet to attain it.

☆

Confusions about work and status and success had their equivalents in the dissatisfactions of sheer consumption. With the restored employment and prosperity of the war and postwar years, Americans bought the essentials, the conveniences and the playthings they had so long craved. Just about as fast as they could, they converted their current incomes, as well as the savings that had financed the costs of Anzio and Iwo Jima, into clothes and houses, station wagons and deep freezers, golf clubs and television consoles. But the brief, joyous flush of acquisition could not obscure the pathos in the lives of those seeking a semblance of success by sending dollars out in chase of goods. Though Keynes was correct about deficits and depressions, a society of men spending their way to status ran directly toward a close facsimile of Orwell's 1984. Obviously the salesmen of fashion had dealt in envy, not in satisfaction.

Yet a sentimental nostalgia alone dignified a subsistence culture. "A man is a beggar who only lives to the useful," Ralph Waldo Emerson had written, and beggars there had to be while the economy commanded the bulk of human energy and the culture condemned an unproductive use of time. Oppressive conformity, Emerson's anathema, did not develop because of abundance. It had reigned in his time, one burden of a community where most men, farmers in particular, worked to exhaustion and lacked the money or the leisure to express their tastes. It reigned still in the United States of the depression and the years that followed it among those Americans without access to professional or remunerative employment. The most visible victims of mere subsistence were the Negroes. Prejudice cost them the chance, however small, for self-fulfillment and the chance, however superficial, for acquiring the components of self-esteem. Most of them were denied the education necessary for uncovering, much less for developing, their talents, and thus denied the right to work in satisfaction. Most of them were denied, too, the jobs that paid salaries large enough for buying comforts and other compensations, while others were denied access to stores and theaters and hotels where they wished to buy, and thus both groups were deprived of the right to work for the semblances of success. On its own terms, even Madison Avenue understood their plight. Negroes, according to one marketing survey, even more than whites, equated much-advertised brands with "prestige, status and equality." "Being husky and rugged," that survey found, "is not particularly attractive to the Negro . . . The kinds of jobs which are available to him, have already demonstrated that he is husky and rugged. Being slim and distinguished is much more preferable." Those characteristics — the pseudo-distinctions of a brand of narrow shoes or of a whiskey trademark pleading gentle birth — connoted success to black and white Americans alike. For all their fraudulence, moreover, the slimming brands at least relieved the monotony of impoverished life for men of any color, and with variety, sometimes provided a touch of elegance or fun.

Exactly as did poverty, however, fashion lacked the capacity to give lasting satisfaction. That quality depended upon an excellence of purpose, of form and execution — upon style — that endured while vogues declined. It was an absence of style that encouraged the costly vulgarity that paraded through Veblen's nightmares. Here advertising, ambassador to vogue, exemplified the problem, for advertising rarely ministered to style. Indeed, by enduring, style rejected the artificial claims of the salesmen of false esteem. Those salesmen, their clients, and the media they employed, displayed small sense of obligation to propose a separation of fashion from esteem, or of status from the image of success. Indeed probably the obligation was not theirs, for neither advertising nor its servants had occasion to renounce the profits of a gospel preached so many years.

Style, in any event, was not susceptible to mass production. The man who recognized it, like the man who created it, did so alone. It was akin to what Emerson meant by genius, the disciplined expression of a creative instinct. Only exploration of the self and of its world disclosed that path to satisfaction. Far better than toil, leisure could help reveal genius and give it vent, could bring a man to build a style of his own.

Leisure, moreover, the most common coin of national plenty, functioned in the postwar years, as it had before, as one medium of inflating opportunity. Transcending the banality of Madison Avenue, Americans seized their chance to spend their wealth for time and tools to use it. There were, most palpably, the power saws in the cellars and the dry flies on the lakes; there were the gardens, the sailboats, the skis, the bedrolls from Albany unfurled in Montana. For hundreds of the growing thousands who acquired them, these were more than diversions, more than toys. They were in some degree instead the instruments of a process allowing a legitimate pride in skill or seeking a renewed rapport with nature. Those satisfactions, neither mean nor silly nor — in the balance — expensive, resembled the very essence of genius, in Emerson's sense of the word.

Other quantities measured different satisfactions. There

were the palettes and pianos, the titles in soft covers, the records, the tents for summer symphony and theater. Never anywhere did intellectuals have larger audiences, the arts more patrons, or patrons wider choice than in postwar America. Leisure and abundance set off an explosion of high culture, and hundreds of the growing thousands who painted or played or listened found both joy and style in the processes of their minds. That represented a genuine success — a success devoid of status and achieved during a leisure curiously akin to work.

The quality of goods and leisure that Americans consumed also advanced. Perhaps there occurred no relative increase in the number of great artists. Certainly ugliness still abounded, and certainly, too, in many quarters a well-cut lawn won much more glory than did well-written sonnets or sonatas. But abundance permitted a discernible education of taste and a mounting demand for beauty. Those changes appeared especially in modern architecture, city planning, and commerical design, less often in the offerings of the movies, television, and the magazines. Still, even the incidental music of the omnipresent westerns acquainted children with subtle harmonies their parents had rejected as discord.

Refinement, as always, proceeded through stages, and the sophisticated, as always, tended to deplore its pace, but pessimism was inappropriate to their meritorious impatience. Culture, as it were, moved in the pattern that George Fitzhugh once ascribed to labor. There lay at the bottom an unavoidable mudsill of slaves to the vulgar and the trite. Yet each cultural quake lifted mudsill and mountain peak alike. As one observer reminded British critics who deplored the horrid and the sham they saw across the ocean, the cultural tribulations of Americans were not theirs alone, but the shared experience of mass society in this century. Compared to other peoples, Americans did rather well. Indeed, under conditions of plenty, conspicuous emulation proved to be an effective agency for communicating gradually the advancing standards of an intellectual elite.

☆

A better agency of communication was education, through which leisure scored its largest triumphs. At the turn of the century illiteracy thrived on child labor. By mid-century both were substantially erased. American children received the spare time to learn to read, though the means they employed sometimes proved inefficient, and the time to go at least through secondary school, though not all of them chose to. Many of the marginally talented found the time and means for college, and more could have, had there been available the necessary public funds and parental motivations.

For all its shortcomings, the national performance in education set significant precedents over fifty years. The prolonging of school attendance, the resulting postponement of career, depended upon a distribution of general wealth in the form of leisure and facilities to individuals of less than average means, including those in communities of less than average standing. Those individuals who labored at that leisure, moreover, confirmed the promise inherent in the fading cult of work. Their productive use of time opened to them opportunities for both kinds of success — for the careers that society esteemed and, more durable though less honored, for the satisfactions that trained minds achieved.

The gospel of work had always made allowance for education as a factor in the success of esteem, for learning, as Franklin had said, was a "natural source of wealth and honor." Though it was the success of satisfaction that meant more to Emerson, education, in school or out, was in his view the dowser for the genius for which he sought release. "Half engaged in the soil, pawing to get free," he wrote, "man needs all the music that can be brought to disengage him . . . If Trade with its money; if Art with its portfolios; if Science with her telegraphs through the deeps of space and time can set his dull nerves throbbing . . . make way and sing." The kind of education he endorsed pointed that way.

Without denying education that task of inspiration, Alfred North Whitehead demanded for it a more definite content and more manifest aim. "Culture should be for action," he wrote in a tone of resonance for Americans. Formal liberal education taught men to act, for it whetted their perceptions and instilled a sense of manner. It taught them style, in Whitehead's phrase "the last acquirement of the educated mind . . . also the most useful." "With style," he held, "you attain your end and nothing but your end. With style the effect of your activity is calculable."

Useful for men who took their satisfaction in their work, style in Whitehead's sense was no less useful for those who sought like rewards in leisure. The very abundance of spare time invited action disciplined by education, action in leisure but no less fulfilling on that account. "Style," Whitehead concluded, "is the ultimate morality of the mind." With it, a new freedom of time made possible a new plenty, not primarily of goods and services, but of creative experiences to set man's dull nerves throbbing, to lift him to Emerson's depths of space and time.

☆

In an age of leisure, the want of a liberal education, the absence of a morality of the mind, could be frightening at worst and at best could lead to drudgery from which one escape was pointless or compulsive work. For those who resisted introspection or self-expression, spare time was anguish, especially when society persisted in unthinking recitations of corollaries to the cult of work. The resulting perplexities disturbed particularly those at or near retirement. Lacking a positive, private mission, most elder men and women suffered from a sense of uselessness that derived from identifying both virtue and success with work. Frequently their anxieties depleted their constitutions as well as their morale. American society was rich enough to support advances in medicine and public health that lengthened life expectancies, and rich enough to provide common, sometimes handsome, pensions. American culture, however, had not developed a corollary gerontology. The aged — those forced to retire whatever their vigor and choice — needed especially to learn the uses of productive leisure.

Adults in middle life fared little better. Contemptuous of their jobs, bored with more pay and more consumption, laborers were alarmed by the pace of automation which constantly reduced the range of interest in most positions, industrial or clerical. To relieve the frustrations of its members, one union gave top priority to programs designed to increase their sensibilities for leisure. Emptiness at work and leisure also affected middle-class women, restless at their chores, their clubs, their volunteer committees for a dozen social services, each with three dozen titled officers. The "dilemma" of modern women, some of them perceived, reflected in part an education geared to careers that were devoid of commitment. So, too, with middle-class men: trained to operate the complex machines, mechanical or organizational, of a sophisticated economy, they quickly reached a ceiling of performance and responsibility beyond which lay tedium and ennui. Such had been their experience as youths during the Second World War when they mastered radar and then sat, despondent, with Mr. Roberts, preferring danger to another night alone. Older, as civilians, they dreaded still to sit alone. Their peacetime radar conquered, they fled from the privacy they feared to another flickering scope or to the empty company of togetherness. There they met their wives, resourceless fugitives from time saved by electricity and prepackaged foods. As their forebears had wasted abundant land and water, so now they wasted leisure.

An advanced technology perforce demanded longer and better schooling of technicians to manipulate its engines and its laws, but a leisure culture required even more. It had to educate its citizens to use their time; it had to teach them a morality of the mind, or else allow them to corrupt their opportunity. In that necessary mission, the shortcomings of American education were especially obvious.

"It is shocking," Walter Lippmann wrote in trenchant indignation, "and indeed something in the way of a disgrace, that this country, which . . . is so rich, has not had the purpose or the will . . . or a sufficiently responsible sense of the future to provide an adequate school system." The federal Commissioner of Education in 1963 reported "one child in every three in public schools . . . culturally deprived." The deprivation was dual. Children attending dilapidated schools with obsolete facilities and harassed, mistrained teachers, could rarely learn enough to qualify for vocations that commanded the status or the income of the middle class. Even rarer was their chance to know the stimulation of the mind essential for finding leisure avocations. That chance was little better in many standard classrooms where the glitter on new equipment faded in dull routines. The substance and the quality of American education too often mocked the promises of Franklin and of Emerson alike.

Slowly public policies supplied correctives. In the decade of the 1950's the states and localities strained their resources to build better schools and to recruit abler teachers. The federal government loitered at that task, blocked by those who urged substandard districts to preserve their freedom to contract with ignorance rather than submit to the alleged corruption of outside help. Yet even that opposition to federal aid allowed support for grants for bricks and mortar or for encouraging science, whose obvious utility for national defense and economic development imparted to it the sanctions of industriousness. Public authorities recognized the need for mobilizing talent and excitement for the sciences, and for retraining labor for the technology of automation — the need to adapt American education to new kinds of work. They stretched their understanding of the right to work to encompass companion rights to earn and spend and play. But their programs left their beneficiaries largely unprepared for leisure, left them still slaves to the useful and the modish and the dull.

It fell therefore primarily to private agencies to demonstrate that a system productive of unparalleled wealth could also cultivate satisfying individuality, to prove that men welcomed freedom from want partly because they valued freedom to discover and express themselves. Adventurous schools and universities, spurred by their staffs and abetted by the rich foundations, moved toward those ends. Following the leads of

Columbia, Chicago and Harvard, collegiate curricula during the 1950's required broader intellectual experiences for all undergraduates. At the better institutions, the life of the mind penetrated the life of the campus, and a leadership of intellectual commitment established approved models of behavior for students who had copied more frivolous examples in prewar years. Intellectuality, not to the exclusion but to the enhancement of other interests, lifted classroom performances and directed leisure to activities involving learning, labor and participation. Staking their prestige on the excellence of the education they offered, elite schools and colleges and universities pulled less richly endowed competitors toward standards satisfactory for national cultural needs.

Scientists, whose work could abide few lazy knaves or scurrying fools, often prodded their colleagues in the arts to those improvements, while both groups were alerted by the need to instruct serious young men and women in branches of scholarship other than their own. The resulting collaborations in educational purpose sometimes produced arresting innovations in emphasis and technique that excited undergraduates at all levels of competence and learning. By 1965 distinguished physicists, mathematicians and biologists had designed imaginative introductions to their disciplines for adoption by the secondary schools, and social scientists and linguists were undertaking similar experiments. The leaven of intellectual excellence promised eventually to lead even marginal students to reaches of learning sufficient not just for respectable employment but for rewarding leisure, too.

☆

For those potentialities the New Frontier supplied significant examples. As its initiative, young Americans volunteered years of their leisure, years subtracted from the span of their careers, for service at the edges of civilization instructing near-primitives in useful work. In the learned and vigorous leisure of government's new personnel and their wives, the arts commanded patronage and respect. The dining room of the White House, the President mused as he looked upon one gathering of distinguished guests, had not contained so much knowledge and versatility at one time since Thomas Jefferson last sat there alone. Nor had the grace of the White House received such thoughtful care, nor had the federal establishment welcomed intellect more warmly.

American experience had long since attested that a rich society, if it so chose, could suffuse its members with fashionable goods, inflate their traffic in purchasable esteem, afford them time to spare in every year at every age. The American performance had indicated at its best that leisure time was susceptible to general use in contemplation or creativity. But American culture had still not endowed leisure with a gospel of confidence, a gospel as powerful and pervasive as the cult of work had once been. That failure stemmed from confusions long embedded in the culture, especially from perversions of the meaning of success. The cult of work too easily mistook labor for character, accumulation for virtue, and both for satisfaction. The cult of consumption for its part mistook fashion for style, comfort for happiness, and acquisition for fulfillment.

Still, in its too rare but splendid moments, the culture of an advanced technology, a leisure culture, recognized obligations to allocate to every man an ample stock of opportunity and plenty. It had also begun to help him reach for dignity, to help him open for exploration the boundless realms of inquiring minds. Primarily through its agencies for education, American society had started teaching the new, the now inclusive leisure class to work — to work to find the private satisfactions so abundant in their plentitude of time. There lay the cradle of Emerson's genius, by which each individual identified himself in just pursuits. There lay the crucible of Whitehead's style, which guided the actions of each differentiated man. Only such men were finally successful, for only they were engaged, only they were fulfilled. In the whole meaning of the national promise, only such men were free.

Chapter
6

★ ★ ★ ★ ★

THE GREATER
CONCEPTION

"THE MYSTERIOUS hopes and fears," in Emerson's phrase, "connected . . . with the name . . . of America" gave the young nation its essential grandeur in the nineteenth-century world. The limitations of the national performance appeared transient, its breadth formidable and expansive. Especially to Americans, but in lesser degree to others, too, no other country exhibited as tangibly as did the United States the growing possibilities for the free self within an open, democratic, plentiful society. No other so vividly represented the expectations associated with independent, self-determined nationality. Confident of the superiority and the attractiveness of their culture, just as sure of the ennui and decadence of the Old World, Americans by and large believed the spread of their revolution — of their systems of government and social organization — to be inevitable. Further, except within the regions bordering on their own continental ambitions, they counted on encouraging inevitability primarily by sympathy and example. That calculation was prompted by the distribution of international power and the direction of international politics.

Those factors gave the United States a near immunity, prolonged, unearned, and precious, from foreign threats or interruptions to the progress of domestic affairs.

The nineteenth century had not ended before the physical and economic wealth of the country made it potentially a major world power. Within little time, that condition of itself generated pressures from without, from would-be friends seeking succor and from would-be rivals seeking gains, that forced Americans to decide either to realize and use their strength or, by neglecting it, to expose their influence and ultimately their security to the inclinations of other strong peoples. From the first, moreover, the potentiality of power persuaded some Americans to attempt to make the nation the deputy of inevitability, to try to employ its wealth and strength to impose American ways elsewhere. That missionary intention, at once unselfish and self-satisfied, demanded an end to political insularity and, in some degree, an assertion of American prestige.

The demand for involvement admitted no final contradiction, for in the eruptive world of the twentieth century there was no escaping the fact and the responsibility of power. The exercise of power and the exigencies of security in their turn precluded trusting foreign relations to sympathy and example alone. Resort to authority and assistance helped to bring the promises of American life closer to other peoples. In those respects, the external circumstances and the suitable instruments of American foreign policy changed without altering the essence of American ideals or the allure of the American symbol abroad. There occurred grave alterations, however, when national policy yielded, as on occasion it did, to the temptations of pride or of self-righteousness. The United States broke its national promise when it placed its own grandeur ahead of the interests of those it helped. It perverted the promise when it followed a course legitimate for its own security in the disingenuous name of someone else's freedom. It violated the promise when it insisted that another country's self-determination adhere to the patterns of the American model.

Within American foreign policy in the twentieth century, tensions arose early and late over whether to use American power, a question to which the needs of national security eventually provided an incontestable affirmative. But tensions arose continually, too, over when and where and how to use American power. To answer those questions, the advices of national security had to be weighed with, and sometimes painfully against, considerations of national purpose. When it held to its heritage, the mature nation, without surrendering its intrinsic interests, endeavored to preserve the connection of mankind's hopes with the name of the United States.

☆

A complex of motives primed the burst of American imperialism of the last years of the nineteenth century. The logic of national defense then fixed the attention of its students on the necessity of military control over the ocean perimeter marked by Alaska, Hawaii, the isthmus of Central America, and the eastern approaches to the Caribbean. The chief proponents of that logic also urged the nation to foster its prestige in the manner of European powers by acquiring colonies and areas of interest in the Pacific and in Asia. Many of them believed, too, as did other Americans, that the United States shared with Europeans a duty to plant western civilization in primitive regions of the world. In that belief, the United States had a supreme colonial mission which in some instances included, to the satisfaction of the national conscience, the liquidation of Old World hegemonies and the substitution of local autonomy under American tutelage. In order to enlist the support of the business community, the imperialists argued, too, with more success than the data warranted, that a lucrative trade would accompany the export of the flag. Taken all together, those motives and contentions led the United States to war with Spain, to the annexation of Hawaii, dominion over Puerto Rico, Guam, and the resistant Philippines, suzerainty over Cuba, and self-appointed, partial and equivocal guardianship of China.

But the various motives were not always compatible. In the Philippines, where other powers would have moved in had the United States stayed away, the American adventure in tutelage and grandeur stretched the country's military commitments beyond existing means or probable will for their support. So, too, in China, where rhetoric exceeded strength; while guardianship in Cuba entailed economic help that some Americans were disinclined to render. No newly subject people, moreover, considered American intrusions wholly desirable or benign. And the very processes of involvement carried the United States into the matrix of European politics which American diplomacy still preferred to disregard. In the consequences, American intentions, no less than the policies they inspired, needed sorting out.

Every hour of reflection convinced the opponents of imperialism, as one of them put it, that "the policies that have made this nation great are . . . sufficient to keep it so." He dreaded the expense and the connotations of keeping a standing army and powerful navy. He deplored the training of a costly class of civil servants to spend their lives "in the government of other men" — men "free and equal" and fit to rule themselves "by the good example of the United States." His entreaty for a little America drew on tradition, but it was as specious as the infatuation with grandeur it attacked. Minimizing the army, navy and civil list had not made the nation great. Rather, great national hopes had had scope for their fulfillment because the balance of foreign military forces and the state of military technology had forestalled designs against the United States. Further, men were neither really free nor really equal, nor capable of imitating the American experience, when they were ignorant and hungry and even savage. There was no clarification of the situation of world power in wishing it away.

☆

The problem was embraced by the large view of American foreign policy to which Theodore Roosevelt, as President, disciplined his earlier jingoism. The Congress and the people, he believed, did not ordinarily take the trouble to think carefully about world affairs. Consequently the nation suffered when it lacked a "great leader, a practical powerful man who cares with all his heart for the game." Roosevelt cared. The range of national defense, as his strenuous sermons defined it, included the Caribbean and the Pacific, but national interest spread over the entire globe, for "the increasing interdependence and complexity of international political and economic relations render it incumbent on all civilized and orderly powers to insist on the proper policing of the world."

The nations that executed that duty commanded Roosevelt's admiration. Europeans and Americans alike, in his opinion, were morally culpable only in so far as they failed to contribute to their own national vigor, to the preservation of a just peace, and to the development of backward regions. The mission of America, as Roosevelt interpreted it, was to join and to excel other nations in those functions. Disdainful of the self-abnegation of American continentalism, he led the United States into the arena of world politics.

The balance of European power at the turn of the century suited him, for it presented no challenge to American interests or to the general peace. But aware of the growth of German ambitions and of the related networks of alliances, he appreciated the severity of the crisis of 1905 over Morocco. He therefore interceded to urge negotiation and to preserve the peaceful status quo that helped to guard American safety. Similarly, when Russia and Japan went to war in 1904, Roosevelt brooded over the "immense possibilities . . . for the future of Asia" where he held "slumbering" China to be of little account and Russia to be crippled by her own lassitude. The equitable treaty he arranged between the belligerents, while disappointing to the Japanese, left "each power," as he reported, ". . . in a sense the guarantor of the other's good conduct." He provided an additional guarantee after detecting a "very slight undertone of veiled truculence" in Japan's objections to American immigration policies. "It was essential," Roosevelt then decided, to send American battleships westward around the world so "that we should have it clearly understood by our own people especially, but also by other people, that the Pacific was as much our home waters as the Atlantic." But a show of force in the practice of diplomacy also justified a reasonable detente, and in an executive agreement with the Japanese he received their pledge to leave the defenseless Philippines alone in return for his implicit recognition of their special interests in Korea and Manchuria. He had acted not to penalize but to caution the Japanese, to remind them of American solicitude for peace in Asia and for their self-restraint.

The balance of world power, protecting peace, released the attention of civilization for a prescriptive but edifying supervision of the rest of the world. Roosevelt welcomed all peoples of power as wardens within their own spheres of influence. As he put it to the British in Egypt, the simple alternative was to "govern or go." That standard he also applied to native administrations. "Korea," he noted, "is absolutely Japan's . . . By treaty it was solemnly covenanted that Korea should remain independent. But . . . the treaty rested on the false assumption that Korea could govern herself well . . . Japan could not afford to see Korea in the hands of a great foreign power . . . Therefore . . . Japan . . . took Korea . . . The Japanese have restored and enforced order, built roads and railways, carried out great engineering works, introduced modern sanitation . . . a modern school system, and doubled the commercial and agricultural output." They had done work "like that done under similar conditions by the chief colonial administrators of the United States, England, France and Germany." Roosevelt approved. "In the interest of all the world," he said, ". . . each part of the world should be prosperous and well policed."

On that basis he assumed full responsibility for keeping order in the Caribbean and keeping other powers out. He demanded the lifting of the German, British and Italian blockade of Venezuela, initiated to force the collection of debts due to Europeans, and later he landed troops in Santo Domingo to ensure the regular payment of that country's debts. He defended the clause in the Cuban treaty that gave the United States the right "to intervene for the preservation of Cuban independence" or the maintenance of a government "adequate for the protection of life, property, and individual liberty." So privileged, he sent American forces to put down an insurrection Cuba was "powerless to quell." He also aided the Panamanian revolution for independence with the argument that Colombia was "utterly incapable of keeping order on the Isthmus" and had not ratified a treaty with the United States "which opened the only chance" for "stability . . . permanent peace . . . and the construction of a canal." Those episodes fell within the general policy Roosevelt announced as a corollary to the Monroe Doctrine. "If a nation," he said, "shows that it knows how to act with reasonable efficiency and decency in social and political matters, if it keeps order and pays its obligations, it need fear no interference from the United States. Chronic wrong-doing . . . may . . . require intervention by some civilized nation, and in the western hemisphere . . . may force the United States . . . to the exercise of an international police power . . . Every nation . . . must . . . realize that the right of . . . independence cannot be separated from the responsibility of making good use of it."

Wherever he interceded, Roosevelt directed American imperialism to goals that the United States had identified with its own nationality. In those areas Americans built facilities prerequisite for economic growth. Under pressure from Roosevelt, Congress granted Cuba important tariff concessions, and the Papacy agreed to a distribution of the broad land holdings of the Catholic Church in the Philippines. Roosevelt's proconsuls laid foundations for sanitation and public health, and for the education of native populations in literacy, agriculture, commerce and self-government. In those and other ways, American rule encouraged and enlarged the native middle class. Colonialism assisted progress toward more open and more plentiful societies, enhanced their ability to manage their affairs, multiplied their opportunities in all pursuits but one — the enjoyment of independence.

Over that exception the Rooseveltian system stumbled, for the revolution and independence of the individual remained, as they had been a century before, conditional on the independence of the society. Where proconsuls governed, no others could feel wholly free, no others could express their full sense of self or dignity. Just as much as Americans, Cubans or Dominicans or Filipinos identified with their own culture, cherished their own heritage, and projected their own expectations in their own nationalisms. They hated imperialism even when they recognized its help. Further, like Roosevelt's critics within the United States, they saw American imperialism for what it was, a denial of the hopes symbolized in the American revolution and the American past. Roosevelt judged accurately that powerful nations had a responsibility for keeping order, but he failed to see the relevance of the opinions of weaker nations then affected. He understood American interests; he was, as he put it, "for saying with a bland smile whatever Nationalism demands," but not when that nationalism expressed the wishes of humble peoples. He honored the obligation of civilized countries to share their endowments with those less favored, but he erred in assuming that benevolence excused a kind of tyranny. The realism of the large view, nec essary in its time and later, and commendable in many ways, sacrificed more than it had to of the spirit of American ideals.

☆

Yet it was possible to underestimate the sanity and benevolence inherent in the large view, as Roosevelt's successors did. Never a "practical, powerful" leader, William Howard Taft tended to trust too much the agency of American business and the sovereignty of law and legal processes, but the state of the world during his tenure and the momentum generated by his predecessor reduced his impact on foreign affairs. The first significant departures, some fanciful, some salutary, from Roosevelt's policies were those of Woodrow Wilson. "The force of America," he believed, "is the force of moral principle . . . There is nothing else for which she will contend." In his view, moral principle forbade imperialism and the strife it engendered. Moral principle also enveloped American constitutionalism and international law. Moved by those formulations, Wilson forced American investors to withdraw from a railroad consortium in China, and geared administration in the Philippines to enlarge the native voice in government and to hasten independence. Though he tried to cultivate similar objectives in the Caribbean, American concern for stability there led him to resort to troops and prefectural bankers in several Latin sovereignties. Wilson's own determination to "teach the South American republics to elect good men" provoked his continual meddling in Mexican politics, most blatantly in two armed interventions that distressed all Mexican factions. Still, his insensibility to the pride of Mexican nationalism was balanced by his sympathy for the democratic goals of the Mexican revolution, including a redistribution of property damaging to American investments. He also held back from actual war. It was not primarily selfishness or bellicosity, but Wilson's opaque passion for "constitutional liberty," for bringing "the light of the justice of God" to shine, that placed the United States in a role which Latin Americans could not readily differentiate from imperialism.

Wilson simply asked too much of the underdeveloped nations he wanted to befriend. Until his time, the United States had followed Thomas Jefferson's doctrine for according formal recognition to foreign governments. "We certainly cannot deny to other nations," Jefferson had written, "that principle wherein our own Government is founded, that every nation has a right to govern itself internally under what form it pleases." Wilson established instead his own, less objective standard. "Just government," he held, "rests always upon the consent of the governed, and . . . there can be no freedom without order based upon law and upon the public conscience and approval." On that basis, in several instances he withheld recognition until he was satisfied that a new administration met his criteria for legitimacy, remote though they were from the traditions, the capabilities, and the choices of many other peoples. Wilson's doctrine constricted their freedom of self-expression, their national genius, rather than enhancing it, and made law more obscure rather than more ethical or practicable.

Different difficulties attended the extension of his doctrine to cover aggression in the Orient. His administration, the first to recognize the new Chinese republic, later warned Japan that the United States would not recognize her gains in China that violated Chinese territorial integrity or American treaty rights. The persuasiveness of that pronouncement hinged in part on its enforceability but the United States was not then equipped or disposed to proceed beyond complaint. Nevertheless, Wilson had at least affirmed American sympathy for independent nationality.

Eager also to be a spokesman for peace, he hoped when war broke out in Europe to confine the role of the United States to neutrality and mediation. He associated national interest intimately with the preservation of neutral rights under "the existing rules of international law." His reading of that law permitted the country to function as an arsenal for Great Britain and France, while it also held German submarines, then novel weapons, to "strict accountability" to traditional and debilitating rules of visit and search. American interests were at stake, and the provisioning of France and Great Britain served them, but the delusions of neutrality confused national policy. Identifying the submarine issue with morality rather than strategy, Wilson built an ideological fortress he could not fail to defend without loss of honor and prestige. In his preoccupation with neutrality, he neglected to prepare himself or his constituents for the war his policy invited. Indeed for several years he attempted no assessment of the causes of the war or of its implications for American security. Further, he never asked himself whether neutrality was morally tenable, whether the United States could play the part of a Switzerland or Sweden without quitting the responsibility of great power.

When Germany chose to push him to war, Wilson, admittedly agonized, explained his decision as he understood it, in absolute and idealistic terms. Those he adopted emphasized not the legalisms of neutrality but his vision of a good world, a world of autonomous nations, spontaneously democratic, at peace with themselves and one another. "Our object," he held, ". . . is to vindicate the principles of peace and justice . . . We have no selfish ends to serve. We desire no conquest, no dominion . . . no indemnities . . . We shall fight for the things we have always carried nearest our hearts — for democracy, for the right of those who submit to authority to have a voice in their own governments, for the rights and liberties of small nations, for a universal dominion of right by such a concert of free peoples as shall bring peace and safety to all nations and make the world itself at last free." Disingenuous about the genesis and probable consequences of the war, Wilson's eloquence raised hopes no peace could fully satisfy. Yet his splendid hyperbole defined goals so deeply connected with the national past that few faithful Americans could reject them.

The desire to attain those goals nursed the illusion that the wrath and brutality of war would end in selflessness and charity. For that eventuality, for a "peace without victory," Wilson proposed his fourteen points, of which eight pertained to territorial adjustments that advanced the principle of self-determination in Europe. Another advocated an impartial settlement of colonial claims with careful attention to "the interests of the populations concerned." In the case of former German colonies, those interests seemed to Wilson to involve progress toward independence under the supervision of small and benign European custodians. During the negotiation of the peace, however, he had to accept various compromises. Some of them related to European boundaries, which in any case could not conform exactly to the dictates of self-conscious nationalities. Others granted colonial trusteeships to victorious major powers, who had planned no less imperial an outcome. But Wilson counted on the League of Nations, the crown of his scheme, to improve the shape of the peace, to modify frontiers within Europe, to hold imperial powers to the "sacred trust" of tending "the well-being and development" of "peoples not yet able to stand by themselves." Once independent, those peoples, like others, would benefit from the provision in the Covenant of the League pledging signatories to "respect and preserve as against external aggression the . . . political independence" of all members. That promise had for Wilson a binding moral force. His conception of internationalism postulated a concert of nationalisms, each differentiated by its own mysterious but democratic genius, each sustaining every other.

Wilson's almost mystical faith presumed too much. Independence, even independence with democracy, did not assure individual freedom in an open and bountiful society. The American performance, which was his transcendent example, had been facilitated by conditions of time and place and heritage not universally reproduceable. Wilson condoned economic terms in the peace treaty that impaired postwar recovery in Europe and in the areas dependent on her help and trade. He excluded from his concert Bolshevik Russia, whose government he deplored and would not recognize, but whose power brooded over the entire world. Indeed whatever its moral force, the League, as the French said, lacked the military strength and the decisiveness needed to deter a bold recalcitrant.

That liability especially bothered Americans of the large view, who also believed that the Covenant deprived the United States of a necessary latitude in foreign policy. If Wilson was insensitive to facts of world power, they were equally so to the virtues of holding power responsible to the consensus of a community large enough to include some dissenters from their own views. They scorned collective means for accomplishing purposes they admired — the superintendence of backward peoples, the policing of the world, the keeping of the peace. Yet they never doubted that the affairs of the world affected the United States, and they were eager to assume the duties of an equal, perhaps a senior partner in a *Pax Britannica et Americana*. Arrogant rather than narrow, they so despised Wilson's treaty that they joined with the obstinate advocates of perpetual American insularity in a successful attack against it.

The case for insularity cherished its own delusions. Its spokesmen believed that bankers and munitions makers had plotted to start the war in Europe and to enmesh the United States. Common to Marxists of all nationalities, that thesis had native roots in the United States among the naïve who blamed a conspiracy of financiers and consolidators for the problems of industrialization. Men of that mind also usually imagined that opposition to war in itself constituted a sufficient national defense. Save in its innocent and exemplary mission, the United States, in their view, owed it to the world to keep aloof from the intrigues of Europe. In the European "blood," they held, were "genes" of centuries of hate, distrust and persecution that perpetuated "irreconcilable conflicts between Old and New World concepts of government and of social and economic life." Indeed virtuous Europeans had fled to America. "The shapes of evil inherent in the Old World system," overwhelming Wilson, dictated corrupt settlements which the United States should censure, not least by immunizing itself from association with Europeans in the League.

That analysis stressed the worst aspects of the Treaty of Versailles, which the Wilsonians hoped the League would meliorate, while it overlooked the national interests of both the United States and the European powers, which proponents of the large view apprehended. Yet the reciprocal antagonisms of the two groups of internationalists prevented their cooperation, countenanced the Senate's defeat of the Treaty and the League, and resigned American foreign policy to the chimera of insularity.

☆

The picture of America that emerged—of a rich and strong nation unwilling to take up a mandate in a troubled region, of such a nation distressed by the prospect of formal association with other countries, of that nation afraid of a moral commitment to condemn aggression — characterized foreign policy for more than a decade. Diplomacy and intervention in the Caribbean area continually assisted American investors and unpopular, unenlightened native regimes. Grand guarantees to China and to stability in the Pacific leaned for execution on an undernourished navy and an inflated colonialism in the Philippines. To the Asian and European powers, Washington tendered pleas for disarmament stripped of assurances of collective punishment of depridations, while with few concessions to the vicissitudes of economic reconstruction, it also demanded regular payment of wartime loans. And in the United States, as elsewhere, the coming of depression intensified economic chauvinism and international distrust. No democratic nation was prepared to contend with the totalitarian dangers of the thirties, but none relinquished sooner or more recklessly than did the United States its apparatus for self-defense or its will for determining optimal circumstances for continuing peace.

The American retreat from world affairs, political and economic, weakened the bases for international peace and prosperity, and thus diminished the possibilities for the independent, democratic development of any people. American insularity opened new opportunities for antidemocratic movements which systematically tried to arrogate to themselves promises that underprivileged nationalities had often associated with American symbols. Marxist doctrine, promulgated with structured order by its Soviet episcopacy, offered men an inevitable, utopian freedom and abundance, to be achieved through revolution of the state and dedication of the self. Its Leninist exegesis, damning imperialism as the self-saving device of capitalism, stirred the nationalistic yearnings of subject peoples whom it enticed to communism. To spur inevitability, Lenin also preached the need for precipitating revolution. His technique of revolution through the organization of a disciplined, conspiratorial, fanatical elite was adopted not only by communists but by those, too, who reached for power in the name of anticommunism. The fascists pledged their revolutions to national glorification, to personal comfort and security, and to the absorption of the individual in the state, a submission they called freedom. Communism and fascism burlesqued the meaning of freedom and delivered abundance primarily to their ruling elites. They also frustrated self-determination — fascism by its unabashed self-aggrandizement; communism by its compliance, within the orbit of Soviet influence, to Russian advantage. But the apathy and the timidity of the democracies, the United States not least, suffered totalitarian excursions in world politics to succeed throughout the thirties, and in succeeding, to win new converts and dominions.

☆

No one better grasped the significance of the battle for men's minds than did Franklin Roosevelt. Preoccupied during his first terms in office by domestic problems and politics, Roosevelt believed that the revitalization of American purpose at home would in itself display a democratic alternative to communism and fascism. He also would have liked to have inspirited foreign policy. He had much of Theodore Roosevelt's sensibility for power without his itch for grandeur; he had, too, Wilson's sympathy for the self-fulfillment of other peoples without his penchant for didacticism. But despite this enlightenment of the President, American foreign policy largely reflected a dominating public and congressional demand for isolation.

Only toward Latin America, which Americans had always considered more a part of their own than of a foreign world, was there effective harmony of purpose between President and people. Roosevelt withdrew the last of the marines from the Caribbean, thus confirming in action the earlier repudiation by the Hoover Administration of Theodore Roosevelt's corollary to the Monroe Doctrine. The United States also gave up its treaty rights to intervene in Cuba and Panama, advanced hemispheric political cooperation, and initiated intergovernmental credits to encourage hemispheric trade, as well as conversations looking toward larger economic aid. After one unhappy episode in Cuba, Roosevelt promptly recognized all kinds of governments when they reached power, and he permitted his ambassador to Mexico to defend that nation's radical programs to redistribute land and wealth, often at the expense of American holdings. As he said, Roosevelt dedicated the United States "to the policy of the good neighbor — the neighbor who resolutely respects himself and . . . respects the rights of others — the neighbor who respects his obligations and respects the sanctity of his agreements in and with a world of neighbors."

The obligations of neighborliness in Europe and Asia lay beyond Roosevelt's authority. Though he asked Congress to give flexibility to American policy, at least to empower the executive to embargo shipments of arms to aggressors, when Congress balked he declined to engage himself in futile legislative battle. The resulting maze of isolationist regulations, designed to prevent the kinds of activities that Congress believed responsible for American involvement in the First World War, had the general effect of restricting the potential supply of American materials to victims of aggression. Accordingly those regulations heartened the fascist powers, discouraged the democracies, and darkened already gloomy negotiations for European disarmament. While eager to help to avert a major war, Roosevelt was as determined as his constituents to keep out if one developed. Alert to that aloofness, European and Asian statesmen further discounted American power.

Discreet recourse to his remaining influence gave Roosevelt little weight in world affairs. At the outset of his administration he formally recognized the communist government of the Soviet Union, hoping thereby to move Russia to a balance of power then tipping toward Germany in Europe and Japan in Asia. Following the precedent set by the Wilson and Hoover administrations, he also withheld recognition of Japanese conquests in China. He found ways, too, to supplement Chinese funds for the purchase of American equipment, and he asked American manufacturers of airplanes and their parts to place a moral embargo on sales to Japan. Even those tepid maneuvers worried the State Department, whose officers counseled caution bordering on appeasement. In some degree they were constrained by the weakness of the American navy, which Roosevelt tried gradually to overcome by prudent requests for appropriations for new ships. Meanwhile his probings for cooperation with Great Britain in Asian and European matters did not pierce the distrust of Prime Minister Chamberlain. Mistrusting American constancy of purpose, Chamberlain at one time considered an entente with Japan and later engineered a capitulation to Germany.

The United States, in the opinion of Roosevelt and men of his mind, could not afford indifference toward erosions of freedom and independence abroad. Yet such indifference was one palpable if unintentional result of isolationist legislation. It shamed the nation, embarrassed its friends and potential allies, and exposed it to the possibility of an ultimate, lonesome vulnerability. Trying to awaken the American people, Roosevelt in 1937 commended to them a "quarantine" against the spreading "epidemic of world lawlessness." War, he warned, "is a contagion . . . It can engulf states . . . remote from the original scene of hostilities. We are determined to keep out of war, yet we cannot insure ourselves against the disastrous effects of war and the dangers of involvement . . . We cannot have complete protection in a world of disorder . . . The will for peace . . . must express itself to the end that nations that may be tempted to . . . violate . . . the rights of others will desist from such a course." At last and at least, that speech reminded Americans of what they wanted to forget — the interest of the nation in a stable world, the necessity of earning liberty and security.

The speech, however, provoked for the most part a surly response, a series of complaints from those unwilling to have their fantasies disturbed. They remained so in spite of the unfolding of Nazi designs. Even after the Second World War began, isolationist congressmen conceded to Hitler's enemies only the privilege of buying American weapons with their own inadequate resources and then transporting those purchases in their own insufficient ships through waters seeded with German submarines. The American awakening began only after the Nazis had overrun most of western Europe. Only then did Congress give serious thought to preparedness for national defense, and even then there was strong opposition to conscription and to the emergency assistance Roosevelt organized for England. Restless though he was with the legacy of American insularity, Roosevelt reined his leadership to his own circumspect estimations of public and congressional tolerances. The logic of events in 1940 and 1941, rather more than his explanations of or answers to it, forced persisting sentiment against war gradually to yield to the realization that the barbarous ambitions of Germany, Italy and Japan imperiled the whole world.

Roosevelt clarified the issues at stake brilliantly. In urging the enactment of the Lend Lease bill of 1941, the measure that brought American strength irrevocably into the struggle, he began by observing that national security was already threatened. So were American principles. Neither liberty nor security permitted acquiescence "in a peace dictated by aggressors and sponsored by appeasers." Rather, the United

States looked forward to a peace based on its own democratic goals, on "the supremacy of human rights," on "a world founded upon four essential human freedoms." Those were freedom of speech and expression, freedom of religion, freedom from want "which will secure to every nation a healthy peacetime life," and freedom from fear, especially the fear of physical aggression. "That kind of world," Roosevelt said, "is the very antithesis of the . . . new order of tyranny which the dictators seek to create . . . To that new order we oppose the greater conception — the moral order."

That greater conception, toward which Roosevelt had been pointing in the four years since his Quarantine speech, promised an international New Deal, a universal freedom in all just pursuits. To his Jeffersonian emphases he appended hope for a plentiful society, and he connected those goals to national independence everywhere. The American example, which he had exalted at home, he now identified with American purpose abroad, for which Lend Lease organized national energy. Further, he related that composite mission to the actual politics of the world, to the physical safety of the United States and of its essential allies. Divesting Wilsonian morality of its innocence, he merged it with the realism of the large view, which he thereby purged of its chauvinism. He gave relevance and practicability to the aspirations he defined, the greater conception that was to inform American war and postwar aims.

☆

Clarification of national motives did not give the United States a free hand in the world. Specific policy decisions had to take into account the sometimes conflicting objectives of the nation's allies and the strategies of the nation's enemies. In pondering those variables, Roosevelt sometimes miscalculated, as any man would have, but he never lost sight of his general goals. Since he would not condone Japanese incursions in China and Southeast Asia, Japanese imperialists had either to attack the United States or abandon their ambitions. Accordingly they attacked, not essentially because Roosevelt provoked them, but because the United States stood in their way and they thought they could prevail. So, too, with the Nazis. But the costly lapse of American alertness at Pearl Harbor was only a prelude to the mobilization of triumphant strength.

While committed to the independence of China, Roosevelt had few illusions about the limp, corrupt and arbitrary government of Chiang Kai-shek. He also had no alternative to supplying financial and military aid to a vital ally, nor had he a proper mandate or sufficient leverage to manipulate Chinese politics, which offered only communism as a poor substitute for Chiang. The strategy of the war, more than any other factor, determined the volume of assistance to China. Resistant to proposals for a formidable overland offensive, resistant, too, to suggestions for domestic reform, Chiang and his Chinese advisers plodded toward their downfall. The attrition of the long war with Japan and the paralysis of the Kuomintang together destroyed prospects for democracy in China. No American policy short of effective dominion over China, and probably not even that, could have served more than to delay the outcome. Roosevelt, constantly disappointed by Chiang, was often exasperated, but of all western statesmen he was nevertheless always the most ardent advocate of China's claim to status among the great powers.

So, too, was he the foremost western champion of anticolonialism in Asia and elsewhere. The war against Japanese and German imperialism, according to American criteria, postulated a war for the liquidation of all imperialism. Roosevelt strained the goodwill of his European allies by his concern for the self-determination of peoples under their rule, those in British India particularly, but also those subject to the Dutch, the Belgians and the French. The United States set a telling example. Congress had earlier granted incipient independence to the Philippines, primarily in order to relieve the nation of the burdens of their economy and their defense. The date for independence had yet to come when American forces led the resistance to Japan's invasion of the islands and later mounted the campaign for their liberation. Going beyond the grant of independence, the United States had established a guarantee that its power would help to protect the Philippines against any challenge. Only that kind of an undertaking gave meaning to the termination of colonial rule.

American arms and American troops played a major role in the liberation of Europe. Roosevelt gave that objective first priority in American strategy, and he therefore welcomed the wartime alliance with the Soviet Union. An essential for victory, that alliance grew out of stalwart Russian resistance to the Nazis. Roosevelt approved neither of communism nor of Russian expansion into Poland and the Baltic states. Indeed the United States did not recognize the puppet Baltic governments, and Roosevelt pressed Russia continually to sponsor genuine Polish independence. To that course he obtained Stalin's pledge at Yalta. "The hopeful assumptions" of that and other wartime conferences, as Winston Churchill later wrote, "were soon to be falsified," but, as he added, "they

were the only ones possible at the time." Neither Churchill
nor Roosevelt sold out to the Russians; rather, Stalin broke his
word, though the others tried hard to persuade him of the desirability of "future world cooperation." Had they done
otherwise, they would themselves have born the blame for
contaminating the grand alliance. Further, Russian power in
eastern Europe allowed the United States little real choice but
a policy of trust. Had Roosevelt agreed to Churchill's proposal for an invasion of Europe on its southern flank, moreover, the strategy would have prolonged the war by perhaps a
year. Probably only a cross-channel invasion in 1943 could
have saved more of Europe from Russian arms, but that operation, for which Stalin pleaded, was postponed because of the
British judgment, doubtless sound, that it could not yet succeed.

Above all, the United States strove to save Great Britain
and Russia from Germany, and to drive the Nazis from the
rest of Europe so that each conquered state could then manage its own political reconstruction. To that end, Washington
recognized and negotiated with the various governments in exile. France posed a special problem. Roosevelt dealt with the
Vichy government, the lackey of the Nazis, primarily in order
to ease the Anglo-American military campaign in Africa. If he
was sometimes abrupt with de Gaulle, in spirit a true ally, the
United States with Great Britain nevertheless furnished most
of the equipment of the Free French and endeavored to assure
that the French people could select the postwar government
they themselves preferred. American plans contemplated a
rapid return of Italy to self-government and a similar condition for Germany following a period of probation and denazi-
fication. The division of Germany into separate zones for mil-

itary occupation presumed a harmony of occupation policies and an eventual federation, neither of which the Soviet Union permitted. Had the Russians honored the spirit of Yalta and Potsdam, defeated Germany, once demilitarized and democratized, would have assumed her place as one united nation among the many of the continent.

Roosevelt's vision of the postwar period was a vision of a world at peace. To keep that peace he counted first upon the United Nations, whose mission he saw as a collective application of the principles of his greater conception. Pursuant to his intention, the charter of the United Nations directed that organization to promote the self-determination of all peoples, including colonial peoples; to protect the sovereign equality of all nations, including small and weak and young nations; to maintain the integrity of all treaties; to cultivate human rights and human dignity, including the health, education, and social progress of all men. For the basic provisioning of war-torn areas, the United Nations Relief and Rehabilitation Administration, drawing mostly on American dollars, was to have an immediate significance. Beyond that, through the International Monetary Fund and the World Bank, whose expenses would also fall most heavily upon the United States, Roosevelt hoped to prevent the financial chauvinism of the prewar years, to facilitate trade, and to provide loans for the reconstruction of war-damaged economies and for the development of backward areas. The moral order would require the devotion of all nations, the great powers especially. To rebuild British industry and commerce, Roosevelt contemplated a postwar extension of Lend Lease, and for the Soviet Union, a large credit to simplify the exchange of her raw materials for American plants and machinery. If he underestimated the costs of his program, if he was too sanguine about the reserve strength of the western allies and the potential goodwill of Russia, he did not expect the forging of a just peace to be automatic or easy, and he did not hesitate to urge the American people to clasp the heroic burdens implicit in their heritage.

☆

American will for that task survived the successive shocks of the postwar years. The cold war altered the conditions to which Roosevelt and most of his countrymen had pinned their hopes. Exhaustion in Europe and revolution in China multiplied the international obligations of the United States, while the extravagant expectations, political and economic, of adolescent societies in the southern hemisphere tried American patience and constancy.

Russian manufacture first of atomic weapons and then of intercontinental missiles banished the physical protection once largely afforded by two oceans, and made American security contingent on the allocation of enormous resources to military technology and armaments. Consequently the temptation to retreat into a gilded "fortress America" beguiled a noisy minority whose influence was strong enough sometimes to bend but less often to warp national foreign policy. There were repeatedly times of confusion, times wasted in pointless recrimination, but in a sequence of taxing crises, American leadership responded on the whole with insight and generosity. Tensions between the needs of national security and the furtherance of national ideals remained, but they were now contained, as they had not been in the interwar period, by the recognition that both goals required continuous, vigorous American participation in world affairs.

An appropriate style was set by Harry S Truman, that middle-class man with middle-class plans in the best American traditions. As he later said, when he made mistakes, they showed. So it was, according to his own admission, with his sudden canceling of Lend Lease; so it was, in the guilt-conscious reflection of many Americans, with his order to drop the atomic bomb; so it was, in the evidence of the consequences, with his transitory parsimony in the defense budget. But his budgets rose barely soon enough; his proconsul in Japan supervised a masterful reconstruction there; and Truman denied to Europe briefly only a tiny fraction of what he later solicited for her benefit. His grace under the pressure of events imbued his applications of a policy of "firm and vigilant containment of Russian expansive tendencies." That policy, as it was most lucidly set forth, decried bluster and superfluous toughness. It called rather for meeting with adequate counterforce the shifting Soviet thrusts. By so doing, the United States, while preserving its own vitality as a free nation, attempted to promote moderation in the Kremlin and eventually "the break-up or the gradual mellowing of Soviet power."

American power could not operate successfully in regions contiguous to the mass of Russian strength, for there intervention would result either in defeat or total war, in vanquished fantasies or in Armageddon. But on the peripheries of the dividing world Truman built up resistance to Soviet threats. With Great Britain no longer able to police the Mediterranean, Truman in 1947 mobilized emergency military and economic assistance for Greece and Turkey so that they might "work out their own destinies in their own ways." Later that year his Secretary of State proposed his bold scheme for the resuscitation of Europe, then still staggering under the devastation of war. "The remedy," George Marshall said, "lies in . . . restoring the confidence of the European people in the economic future of their own countries and of Europe as a whole . . . Our policy is directed not against any country or doctrine but against hunger, poverty, desperation and chaos. Its purpose should be the revival of a working economy in the world so as to permit the emergence of political and social conditions in which free institutions can exist . . . The initiative . . . must come from Europe. The role of this country should consist of friendly aid . . . and support."

That extraordinary offer, rejected by Soviet-dominated states, inspired fourteen free nations to form the Organization for European Economic Cooperation which, with American help and over twelve billion dollars of American aid, planned and executed the economic recovery of its members. As Marshall had predicted, with recovery, democratic institutions thrived. Indeed within a decade most Marshall Plan countries, including the German Federal Republic which had been asked to join them, had shown a capacity for hard work, a vigilance for freedom, and a potentiality for abundance. Not through imitation, but through their own performance, they were constructing the good society of American aspirations.

Recovery had not yet begun when the Soviet Union tried to obtain an exclusive hold on Berlin by blocking overland access to that city from the western occupation zones in Germany. Unwilling either to submit or to risk war by dispatching armed convoys, the United States, with help from Great Britain, flew into West Berlin thousands of tons of supplies daily until the blockade was lifted, nearly a year later. The Berlin crisis, and the communist takeover in Czechoslovakia that preceded it, together persuaded the western European democracies to organize for their own mutual defense, in which the United States quickly joined. The members of the resulting North Atlantic Alliance deemed "an attack against one or more of them in Europe or North America . . . an attack against them all." NATO completed the pattern of American engagement in Europe. American funds, American troops and American intelligence invigorated the individual independence and the collective freedom and prosperity of the West, from which the United States gained proportionately to the strength and resolve of its allies. Truman and his associates led the nation to a mutuality with Europe, an interdependence of power and purpose that gave sinew to Roosevelt's vision.

In Asia Truman also attempted to make containment a vehicle for vitality. The invasion of South Korea by the North Korean communists incurred his immediate retaliation with American forces, the first and largest to support the United Nations' condemnation of the aggression. The Korean War involved the prestige of the United Nations and the independence of South Korea, worthy objectives. Truman perhaps erred in letting their importance move him to order American units to cross into North Korea. The temporary tactical gains there mattered less in the end than the political disadvantages of the counterinvasion and the strategic liabilities of the Communist Chinese intervention it helped to provoke. Yet Truman, firm in his opposition to outright war with China, sufficiently confined the operation to make possible ultimately a negotiated peace on the basis of the *status quo ante*, a peace that accomplished the war's original ends. Still, the cost of life and money disturbed the American people who did not clearly grasp the significance of the stakes, superficially limited but essentially grand. Further, in preserving South Korean independence, the United States found itself in the unavoidable but disconcerting position of sustaining the wretched government of Syngman Rhee.

Then and later, the connection between independence and democracy was only tenuous in Asia and in Africa. The United States heckled its allies to release their colonies and stretched its resources to block Chinese expansion, but the beneficiaries of those policies were several generations removed from the political experience and economic sophistication essential for establishing standards of freedom and plenty consonant with those of the West. Their indignant memory of imperialism, their jealousy of Europe and America, their naïveté and impoverishment made the new nations of Asia and Africa peculiarly susceptible to communist blandishments. Undeterred, Truman realized that the best chance for American hopes lay in stimulating economic growth by extending technical assistance to regions still almost primitive. That "bold new program for making the benefits of . . . scientific advances and industrial progress available," as Truman said, assured no "quick solutions," but there would have been "no solutions at all" had not the United States pressed forward "to help these countries grow and flourish in freedom."

☆

The decision of the Republican Party, the sanctuary of loitering isolationism, to nominate Dwight D. Eisenhower, an internationalist candidate, assured continuity in American foreign policy after 1952. His intentions as President accorded with his achievements as a soldier in command of the European theater during the Second World War and of NATO forces thereafter, achievements of fortitude in the cause of decency. Yet Eisenhower had neither a Rooseveltian temper for hearty leadership nor a Wilsonian talent for limpid phraseology. For a sorry season he let foreign policy defer to the vindictive absurdities of the McCarthyites. His Secretary of State then fulminated about liberating eastern Europe, where the United States had no effective power, and unleashing Chiang Kai-shek, who was harnessed by his own futility. That posturing succeeded only in encouraging the vain bravery of the Hungarian revolt. The fustian self-righteousness of American diplomacy, its vacillations in Egypt and its arrogance toward London, primed the environment for the invasion of Suez. Surprised and grieved, Eisenhower defended the integrity of Egypt, a neutralist power leaning left, upheld the principles of the United Nations, and helped to enlist it in the pacification of the dispute. Redeeming another situation for which he was partly responsible, he clarified talk about "massive retaliation," which had sometimes implied only an easy escalation from minor crises to thermonuclear war, and he held American support of communist-threatened nations in Southeast Asia to conventional tactical weapons. In his latter years in office he commended economic assistance for them and for various neutralist and even communist countries needing it. He stepped up the defense program, which had been lagging, while he warned Americans against reverence for the importunities of "the military-industrial complex," which had been greedy. He strove, too, for more rapport with Soviet Russia, then intermittently receptive. In the end, Eisenhower perpetuated the policy of containment and preserved the legacy of purpose it was conceived to protect.

☆

American policy faltered most conspicuously in the western hemisphere. As poverty increased in most Latin American countries, so did the allure of communism, native or imported. The unashamed oppressiveness of most Latin American governments worked to the same result. Yet here, as in so many parts of the world, the United States confronted a dilemma. It could grant military and economic assistance to the ineffective and autocratic governments in being, or by withholding aid, it would seemingly countenance human desperation and certainly perpetuate weakness against upheaval. The sovereign pride of the Latin Americans precluded outright intervention in their domestic affairs, while clandestine activity resembled the communist tactic that the United States officially deplored. Truman and Eisenhower chose to send weapons to rightist dictatorships. The economic help they arranged for Latin America fell short of the continent's needs and profited mainly the small minority of rich men who were often simultaneously removing their own wealth from investment in their native countries to havens in Europe. Consequently the bitterness that Latin Americans felt for their rulers spilled over against the United States, venting itself in the mob violence that greeted Vice President Nixon and, more ominously, in the Castro revolution in Cuba.

In Cuba both the dilemma of American policy, and the related tension between the necessities of national security and the counsel of national ideals, reached an apogee. Cuba, always within the immediate perimeter of American defense, long an important strategic base for American forces, had progressed economically under the impetus of American investment, developing in the process a substantial middle class, hopefully a base for social and political democracy. Under Fulgencio Batista, however, the mass of Cubans shared neither in the island's wealth nor in their own self-government. The Batista dictatorship was in all respects comparable to despotic regimes in various other nations with which the United States, earlier and later, formed defensive alliances. Like his counterparts, Batista used the arms he received to suppress internal opposition and to frustrate internal reform. Consequently the United States was attached indirectly to the side of a miserable status quo. Uncomfortable in that role, Washington cut off aid to Batista before his collapse, and later quickly recognized the Castro government, hailed its initial reforms, and offered it economic assistance. But Castro, whose retinue included some communists, spurned that assistance, turned Cuba into a Russian satellite, sent the moderates in his ranks to death or exile, and sponsored a campaign of subversion throughout Latin America.

At that juncture, the new Kennedy Administration proposed for Latin America the Alliance for Progress, which was designed to speed economic aid, to raise standards of living, and to advance social reform, but tangible gains were predictably slow in materializing. Kennedy also, again without consistent success, attempted to use the prospect of American assistance and the prestige of American recognition to strengthen democratic elements in the hemisphere. More precipitantly, he encouraged a band of anti-Castro Cubans, who had begun training under the auspices of the Eisenhower Administration, to venture their abortive invasion at the Bay of Pigs. That affair, and the American boycott that followed it, fanned Castro's rancor, while his victory fed the insolence that prompted the installation of Soviet jets and offensive missiles in Cuba. Now Kennedy, outraged but steady, ordered an immediate quarantine of further Soviet arms shipments, demanded the dismantling of the missile sites, and warned that he would interpret any attack on the hemisphere from Cuba as the responsibility of Russia and would retaliate accordingly. The Organization of American States endorsed that stand, which also elicited the approval of the NATO nations. Russia removed her weapons. But Cuba remained under Castro, and Latin America in turmoil.

☆

The episode, along with many others, revealed both the efficacy and the limits of national power. The United States had military strength, which the Kennedy Administration rationalized and diversified, and had the will to use it if necessary. Americans and their allies had succeeded in containing the Soviet Union. They had also helped emerging nations toward economic growth, which was augmented, as was the self-respect of the beneficiaries, by the sophistication of Kennedy's aid programs. But the United States, short of drastic intervention indistinguishable from imperialism, could not overcome the tendency among new Asian and African states for neutralism, for debilitating quarrels among themselves, and for Marxist types of social organization — developments that derived from their own cultures and their own readings of their self-interest. Nor could the United States prevent the occasional surrender of a state, even in the Caribbean, to outright communism, or the persistence of rightist tyrannies in

Southeast Asia and Central and South America. Shifts in American support hastened the overthrow of Rhee in South Korea, Boun Oum in Laos, and Diem in Vietnam, but their successors were not paragons of democracy, and other shifts in American support accomplished very little in Haiti, Honduras and the Dominican Republic. A liberal foreign policy understood the immorality of native despotisms, poor substitutes even for colonialism. A realistic policy comprehended the unwillingness of men to fight to sustain oppressive governments, unattractive alternatives to communism. But realism also reckoned with ceilings on resources and commitments, already extended, while liberalism recognized the quiet virtue of self-restraint. Truman had been right about the dark continents; there were no instant or effortless solutions, but eventual prosperity, eventual human liberty, satisfying self-determination depended both on the continuance of technical and economic aid and on the diligence of its recipients.

The very success of the policy of containment recommended reassessment of the techniques appropriate to American purpose. In the aftermath of the Cuban crisis, the anticipated results of containment were increasingly visible both in the rift in Sino-Soviet relations and in the softening of Soviet temper. Advocates within the communist bloc of "peaceful coexistence," the Russians, by their own account, were jealous alike of their prestige and their comforts. There was room for negotiation between the boundaries set by their national pride and by their individual appetites. Within that space lay new opportunities for approaching the goals of the greater conception, as Franklin Roosevelt had hoped to, through cooperation rather than hostility. Dependent primarily on the Russian mood, that chance also rested partly on American willingness to disengage the grandeur of the United States from policies contrived for hostility, a willingness expressed in continuing discussions of disarmament, in a new agreement limiting atomic testing, and in a fresh proposal for joint exploration of outer space. Well before the thaw in the cold war, American programs for aid and trade with several communist states had nursed centrifugal nationalisms within the Soviet orbit. With that thaw, Americans had to consider the kinds of conditions they would accept as sufficient for renewing diplomatic and commercial relations with China and Cuba.

The success of containment, the rupture within the communist bloc, and the ebullience of the European economy reduced the unifying urgency but not the strategic importance of the western alliance. The common interests of the NATO nations competed with the separate interests of various partners whose preferences for joint policy increasingly challenged American guidance. To the dismay of the United States, the European Common Market, child of the Marshall Plan, excluded Great Britain. That decision reflected the influence of renascent France no more than the difficulties of reconciling the welfare of the continental economy with that of the British Commonwealth. Both France and Great Britain, moreover, questioned the efficacy of American policy toward Cuba, China and Vietnam, and refused to imitate it. In matters of joint defense, if French hauteur impeded American plans, the United States, with perhaps more wisdom but no more grace, tended to inform rather than to consult the French about weapons systems, and denied Great Britain types of arms previously promised her. In relations with their friends in Asia as well as in Europe, Americans had to discard the obsolete assumption that their voice in common affairs was by right proportional to their current or past contribution to common strength.

However disparate in wealth and power and wisdom, the partners to the alliance were equal in dignity, as were also the members of the United Nations and the Organization of American States. Otherwise Franklin Roosevelt's plea for self-respect was lost in self-conceit. Yet like other men, Americans were slow to admit their own fallability or to endure presumptuousness in others. After sixty years they had yet fully to eliminate the indignities to Panama incorporated in the treaty governing the canal zone there. Twenty years after the ratification of the United Nations Charter, many of them had yet to adjust to the eventuality of being outvoted by small, sometimes petty, sometimes foolish states. The fancies of grandiosity and insularity were still sustained by the pains of internationalism and the strains of national security. But the blemishes in the American record signified not the failure but the trials of the national performance.

The greater conception ruled American foreign policy. Its makers had forsaken the pursuit of safety in weakness and of peace in retreat. They had dispelled the notion of European corruption and American innocence, and rejected the practice of tutelage by passive example or imperial might. Since Franklin Roosevelt's time, conditions had changed, and with them American tactics, but the objectives of his moral order were the objectives of John F. Kennedy two decades later. "We dare not forget," he said, ". . . that we are the heirs of . . . revolution . . . To those new states whom we welcome to the ranks of the free, we pledge our word that one form of colonial control shall not have passed away merely to be replaced by a far more iron tyranny . . . To those people in the huts and villages of half the globe, struggling to break the bonds of mass misery, we pledge our best efforts to help them help themselves . . . not because the Communists may be doing it . . . but because it is right . . . To . . . the United Nations our best hope in an age where the instruments of war have far outpaced the instruments of peace, we renew our pledge of support . . . Finally, to those nations who would make themselves our adversary, we offer . . . a request; that both sides begin anew the quest for peace." And beyond words, the measures of American striving were many — the imposing generosity of one hundred billion dollars of foreign military and economic aid, the support of United Nations posses to keep the peace, the dangerous and expensive custodianship of deterrence.

The constituents of American hope and vitality were at once the dependents and the guardians of national purpose abroad. There, as at home, the best name of America was connected to scope for personal fulfillment, range for individual freedom, and potentiality for social abundance. When bereft of those purposes, as they sometimes regrettably were, national engagements overseas exchanged authority for force and nobility for pretentiousness. But in more effective cases, heroic aspirations, while in themselves no insurance against error and sorrow, at once guided and magnified American power. To the nation as to its citizens, they also supplied energy, courage, and incomparable style.

Acknowledgments
and Sources

Index

ACKNOWLEDGMENTS
AND SOURCES

AT THE ASPEN INSTITUTE of Humanistic Studies for Executives, in 1958 when I was first invited to serve there as a moderator for a two-week seminar, I discovered to my surprise, after I had arrived, that the director of the institute had scheduled a one-hour lecture in which I was to speak to the topic: "History, the Social Sciences, and the American Contribution to Ideas." That extraordinary assignment, doubtless contrived to permit me a free hand, first alarmed me and then provoked me to organize a rough outline from which this book ultimately developed. An early version of what is now much of chapter four and part of chapter two served as my contribution to Robert E. Spiller and Eric Larrabee, eds., *American Perspectives* (Harvard University Press, Cambridge, 1961). A preliminary statement of a section of chapter five appeared in Clarence Morris, ed., *Trends in Modern American Society* (University of Pennsylvania Press, Philadelphia, 1962). The publishers of those volumes have kindly consented to let me use those essays again here.

At one time or another between 1958 and 1965 every chapter of this book went through several revisions, usually in response to suggestions from audiences to which I had been asked to lecture. Several of those audiences consisted of executives of the American Telephone and Telegraph Company or the General Electric Company; others were gathered at Brown University, the Hartford College for Women, Hollins College, and the University of Pennsylvania; still others were my hosts abroad. For their considerate hospitality and for the amicable criticism of their students, faculties and guests, I am particularly indebted to the University of Munich, the University of Oslo, Oxford University, the Queen's University at Belfast, and above all Cambridge University where I was Pitt Professor of American History and Institutions during the academic year 1963-64. In that pleasant and rewarding period, in six public lectures and several private ones, I brought this book to its penultimate form.

I owe even more to my colleagues Edmund S. Morgan and C. Vann Woodward, and to my editor Craig Wylie, for corrections and suggestions incorporated in the final draft of this book, and for their patience with my rejection of some of their thoughtful counsel. No one of those three good friends either wholly agrees with what I have written or wholly approves the way in which I have expressed my thoughts. Neither does Joan D. Blackmer, who gladly typed the last draft of the manuscript when she would have preferred more vigorous and rewarding exercise, or my wife, who had to listen too often to too many drafts of the book, and did so with her invariable and sustaining grace.

In the paragraphs that follow I have tried to indicate my most pressing obligations to the many historians on whose work I have relied for data and for inspiration. Since the major draft of this book was written in England, I used editions available there, and I have cited the editions I used, many of them reprints. Yet I cannot have said enough, for the effort to write briefly and selectively about some two centuries of American history led me to draw constantly upon the accumulated scholarship of more men than I can conveniently name. Further, I have long benefited from the conversation and advice of wise and generous historians who have not seen the manuscript of this book but who nevertheless contributed indispensably to what I put into it. They will recognize their influences, as well as some respectful disagreements with their points of view. The references below give far less than just credit to Alfred D. Chandler, Jr., Oscar Handlin, Richard Hofstadter, Richard W. Leopold, David M. Potter, Arthur Schlesinger, Jr., and particularly Elting E. Morison whose sensibility for the meaning and the writing of history reflects his matchless perception about the possibilities of man.

☆

CHAPTER I. THE MYSTERIOUS HOPES AND FEARS

My treatment of men in tandem with men-as-metaphors throughout this book both derives and deviates from five significant studies: Marcus Cunliffe, ed., *The Life of Washington by Mason L. Weems* (Cambridge, 1962); Richard Hofstadter, *The American Political Tradition and the Men Who Made It* (New York, 1948); Merrill D. Peterson, *The Jefferson Image in the American Mind* (Galaxy Ed., New York, 1962); John William Ward, *Andrew Jackson — Symbol for an Age* (Galaxy Ed., New York, 1962); and Dixon Wecter, *The Hero in America* (Ann Arbor Ed., Ann Arbor, 1963). For the quotation in the first paragraph of this chapter I am indebted to a reference to John Adams by Arthur Schlesinger, Jr., in a manuscript copy of his Harcourt Lecture at Columbia University. The quotations from Franklin, Jefferson, Hamilton and Emerson I drew respectively from Henry S. Commager, ed., *The Autobiography of Benjamin Franklin and Selections from His Writings* (New York, 1944); Adrienne Koch and William Peden, eds., *The Life and Selected Writings of Thomas Jefferson* (New York, 1944); Samuel McKee, Jr., ed., *Alexander Hamilton's Papers on Public Credit, Commerce and Finance* (Liberal Arts Press Ed., New York, 1957); and Brooks Atkinson, ed., *The Complete Essays and Other Writings of Ralph Waldo Emerson* (New York, 1940). For texts of major pronouncements like Washington's "Farewell Address" and the Monroe Doctrine, I referred, for all chapters of this book, to *The People Shall Judge*, 2 vols. (University of Chicago Press, Chicago, 1949). In this and other chapters, my discussion of abundance owes much to David M. Potter, *People of Plenty* (Chicago, 1954). The reading of Emerson throughout the volume rests often upon conversations with the late Perry Miller, and on Daniel Aaron, *Men of Good Hope* (New York, 1951).

CHAPTER II. THE ENERGY OF THE NATION

The discussion of industrialism and industrialists follows paths first cleared for me by Edward C. Kirkland, *Business in the Gilded Age* (Madison, 1952) and *Dream and Thought in the Business Community, 1860-1900* (Ithaca, 1956), and by Alfred D. Chandler, Jr., *Henry Varnum Poor* (Cambridge, 1956) and *Strategy and Structure* (Cambridge, 1962). Thomas Mellon is quoted from his privately printed autobiography, *Thomas Mellon and His Times* (Pittsburgh, 1885); the quotations from Andrew Carnegie are from his *Autobiog-*

raphy (Boston, 1920). For my treatment of the political creed of the industrialists and its social and legal ramifications, I am obliged particularly to the advice of Alexander M. Bickel and to Robert G. McCloskey, *American Conservatism in the Age of Enterprise* (Cambridge, 1951) and Arnold M. Paul, *Conservative Crisis and the Rule of Law* (Ithaca, 1960). My remarks about the farmers and other reformers drew heavily on C. Vann Woodward, *Tom Watson, Agrarian Rebel* (New York, 1938) and on *The Chicago Conference on Trusts* (Chicago, 1899).

CHAPTER III. A MIDDLE-CLASS COUNTRY

In working through the magazines cited in the text of this chapter, I was assisted by Kathleen Pasch. The interpretations in the chapter reflect the influence above all of the voluminous writings of Oscar Handlin, but also of Robert A. Dahl, *Who Governs?* (New Haven, 1961); Richard Hofstadter, *The Age of Reform* (New York, 1955); George E. Mowry, *The Era of Theodore Roosevelt* (New York, 1958); William V. Shannon, *The American Irish* (New York, 1963); and C. Vann Woodward, *Origins of the New South* (Baton Rouge, 1951).

CHAPTER IV. TO RESTORE THE ANCIENT TRUTHS

In this chapter, as in parts of the preceding one, I have leaned on and occasionally quoted from earlier books of my own, among them *Joe Tumulty and the Wilson Era* (Boston, 1951); *The Republican Roosevelt* (Cambridge, 1954); *Woodrow Wilson and the Politics of Morality* (Boston, 1956); and *Yesterday's Children* (Boston, 1959). That work in turn owed a particularly large debt to Richard W. Leopold, Arthur S. Link, and Elting E. Morison. In the latter parts of this chapter, and in parts of the next, I profited from William E. Leuchtenburg, *Franklin D. Roosevelt and the New Deal* (New York, 1963); Eric F. Goldman, *The Crucial Decade — and After* (Vintage Ed., New York, 1961); and especially Arthur M. Schlesinger, Jr., *The Age of Roosevelt*, 3 vols. (Boston, 1957-1960).

CHAPTER V. THE ULTIMATE MORALITY

The cult of work of the 1920's imbues Bruce Barton, *The Man Nobody Knows* (Pocket Book Ed., New York, 1941), and is admirably explicated in James W. Prothro, *The Dollar Decade* (Baton Rouge, 1954). My remarks about advertising were inspired largely by Otis Pease, *The Responsibilities of American Advertising* (New Haven, 1958) and also by Martin Mayer, *Madison Avenue, U.S.A.* (Pocket Book Ed., New York, 1959). There are brilliant insights about work in Daniel Bell, *The End of Ideology* (Collier Books Ed., New York, 1961). No one has discussed the limitations of conventional economic wisdom as well as John K. Galbraith, *The Liberal Hour* (Boston, 1960). The *New York Times*, in its engaging daily column about advertising, reported the advertising survey about Negroes. On questions relating to education, I have obviously turned to Alfred North Whitehead, *The Aims of Education* (Mentor Ed., New York, 1955) and to the many accomplishments of Educational Services, Inc., along with its guiding intelligences and their writings, especially Jerome S. Bruner, *On Knowing* (Atheneum Ed., New York, 1965).

CHAPTER VI. THE GREATER CONCEPTION

The acknowledgments for Chapter IV apply here as well. The phrase "unearned security" I first met in Walter Lippmann, *U. S. Foreign Policy: Shield of the Republic* (Boston, 1943), where it is redolent of certain attitudes of Theodore Roosevelt. There is an earlier use of the phrase and the ideas it connotes in Franklin Roosevelt's "Four Freedoms" address, quoted in part in the text of this chapter. C. Vann Woodward gave a later but wholly original usage to the phrase "free security," to which he lent connotations of his own. The anti-imperialist quoted early in this chapter is George F. Hoar. The quotation about European "blood," and the connected ideas, are from Herbert C. Hoover, *The Ordeal of Woodrow Wilson* (New York, 1958). For data on American foreign policy since 1938 I am indebted to many authors, no one of whom would find my interpretations fully satisfactory. The two works that have influenced me most on the subject are the unpublished Commonwealth lectures of Arthur Schlesinger, Jr. on Franklin Roosevelt, and Walt W. Rostow, *The United States in the World Arena* (New York, 1960). Both authors have been equally persuasive in various conversations, though they do not entirely agree with each other or with me. As the content of the chapter reveals, I have also much admired the papers and addresses, and the creativity and adaptability in policy making, of George F. Kennan. Finally, the chapter was improved by discerning suggestions of William R. Emerson.

INDEX

Adams, Brooks, 70, 71
Advertising, 129-132, 138-139
Agriculture. *See* Farmers
Alger, Horatio, 45, 127
Alliance for Progress, 184
American Federation of Labor, 99
American Law Review, 52
American promise: defined, 15; impact on Europe, 16
American Review of Reviews, 71
American Revolution: Jefferson's view of, 9
Argentina, 16
Atlantic, 71

Bagehot, Walter, ix
Batista, Fulgencio, 184
Bay of Pigs invasion, 184-185
Bellamy, Edward, 58
Berlin Blockade, 179-180
Brady, John Green, 66-67
Brandeis, Louis D., 88, 93
Brewer, David J., 51
Bruner, Jerome, x
Bryan, William Jennings, 74, 85, 113
Bryce, Lord, 106

Business: Emerson's view of, 23-24
Business cycle, 35-36

Carnegie, Andrew, 36, 45, 46, 55, 81, 85; career of, 40-43
Castro, Fidel, 183, 184, 185
Chamberlain, Neville, 170
Chemical industry, 33
Chiang Kai-shek, 173, 182
China: American guardianship of, 154; Theodore Roosevelt's view of, 156; and Woodrow Wilson, 160, 161; policy after World War I, 166; and Franklin Roosevelt, 173; policy after World War II, 187
Churchill, Winston, 117, 174-175
Civil War, 25-26, 54
Cohan, George M., 81
Cold War: and foreign policy, 177-178
Colleges: changes in curricula, 145-146
Colombia, 16, 158
Communism, 167. *See also* Russia

Consumption: after World War II, 137
Coolidge, Calvin, 111-112, 113, 127
Corbett, James, 83
Corporations. See Industrialization; Industry, Consolidation of
Coughlin, John, 83
Crockett, Davy, 20
Cuba, 154, 187; and Theodore Roosevelt, 158; and Franklin Roosevelt, 168; Castro revolution in, 183-185
Culture, 140-141, 147
Czechoslovakia, 180

Darwin, Charles, 41
Davis, Robert, 83, 84, 85, 86, 87
Declaration of Independence, 9
Democratic Party: in the 1920's, 110-111
Depression of the 1930's, 112-113, 132-133
Dominican Republic, 186
Du Bois, W. E. B., 92, 93

Economic conditions: early 20th century, 64-65
Economic growth: Hamilton and, 11-14; and national purposes, 58-59
Edison, Thomas, A., 38
Education: Franklin on, 5-6; Jefferson on, 7-8; and industrial consolidation, 44-45; gifts of wealthy to, 72-73; in 20th century, 141-146
Egypt, 182
Eisenhower, Dwight David, 120; foreign policy of, 181-183
Electricity, 32, 33
Eliot, T. S., x
Emerson, Ralph Waldo, 53, 57, 63, 139, 148, 151; on poets, ix; as poet laureate, 21; and Franklin, 22; and Jefferson, 22; and Hamilton, 23; and business, 23-24; and the Negro, 24; and Lincoln, 24, 25, 27; and the Civil War, 31; on conformity, 137; on education, 142
Engineering, 44-45
Ethnic groups. See Prejudice, ethnic and names of specific groups
Europe: effect of American promise on, 16
European Common Market, 187

Fair Deal, 119
Farmers: and industrial consolidation, 56-57, 98-99; desire for middle class life, 76-77; increasing efficiency of, 78-79; under New Deal, 115; after World War II, 118
Farmers' Union, 79
Fascism, 167
Federal aid to education, 145
Federal Art Project, 135
Federal Theater Project, 135
Federal Writers Project, 135
Fitzgerald, John F., 83
Fitzhugh, George, 140
Ford, Henry, 126
Foreign policy: and national purpose, 152-153; under Theodore Roosevelt, 155-160; under Woodrow Wilson, 160-165; after World War I, 166-168; under Franklin Roosevelt, 168-177; under Truman, 178-181; under Eisenhower, 181-183; under Kennedy, 184-189
France, 175, 187
Franklin, Benjamin, 11, 14, 18,

Franklin, Benjamin, *cont'd:*
    41, 70, 72; and work, 4-5, 126,
    128; and education, 5, 142; as
    symbol of success, 6; and Emer-
    son, 22; and Lincoln, 25
French Revolution, 8
Frick, Henry C., 46

General Motors Corporation, 130
George, Henry, 58, 74, 85
German-Americans, 87
Germany, 17, 175-176
Gibbons, James Cardinal, 81
Great Britain, 16, 175, 178, 187
Greece, 16, 178
Guam, 154

Haiti, 186
Hall, Lt. J. Lee, 70
Hamilton, Alexander, 16, 18, 32,
    93; career of, 10-14; and An-
    drew Jackson, 20; and Emer-
    son, 23; and Lincoln, 25
Harper's Weekly, 71, 73
Harvard College, 72
Hawaii, 154
Heath, Perry Sanford, 69-70
Hill, David Jayne, 70
Hitler, Adolf, 171
Hobbes, Thomas, 36
Holding companies, 37
Holmes, Oliver Wendell, Jr., 53
Homestead strike, 56
Honduras, 186
Hoover, Herbert, 113, 128-129
Hungary, 17, 182

Immigration: restriction of, 102
Imperialism, 153-155, 158-160.
    See also Foreign policy
Income tax, 52-53, 103; and New
    Deal, 116-117
Independent, 67, 71, 73; its sur-
vey of the middle class, 64-65;
    on gifts to education, 72-73
Indians, American, 73
Industrialization, 32-39; and na-
    tional ideals, 46-47; and gov-
    ernment, 47-49; and the courts,
    49-50. *See also* Economic
    growth; Farmers; Labor
Industrial Workers of the World,
    90
Industry, consolidation of, 36-39,
    43-44
International Bank for Reconstruc-
    tion and Development, 176
International Monetary Fund, 176
Interstate Commerce Commis-
    sion, 52
Ireland, Archbishop John, 81
Irish-Americans, 79-87
Italian-Americans, 88
Italy, 16

Jackson, Andrew, ix, 19-20, 32,
    56, 113
Japan: and Theodore Roosevelt,
    156-157; and Woodrow Wil-
    son, 161; and Franklin Roose-
    velt, 169-170; and Truman, 178
Jefferson, Thomas, 11, 14, 17, 18,
    45, 52, 54, 72, 113, 147; on
    freedom and land, 6-7; on edu-
    cation, 7-8; and French Revolu-
    tion, 8; and politics, 8; and
    American Revolution, 9; heroic
    role of, 10; and Emerson, 22;
    and Lincoln, 25; and 19th-cen-
    tury farmers, 56; and foreign
    affairs, 161
Jews in the U.S., 87-88
Johnson, Lyndon B., 121

Kenna, Michael, 83
Kennedy, John Fitzgerald: and

Kennedy, John Fitzgerald, *cont'd*: the American promise, 120-121; foreign policy of, 184-189

Keynes, J. M., 134, 137

Knapp, Seaman A., 78, 93

Korea: and Japan, 157

Korean War, 180-181

Labor: and industrial consolidation, 57, 99-100; under New Deal, 115; after World War II, 118

Lambs' Club, 81

Laos, 186

Latin America: effect of American promise on, 16; and Franklin Roosevelt, 168-169; after World War II, 183-185

League of Nations, 164-166

Lehman, Herbert, 88

Lehman, Irving, 88

Leisure, 125; after World War II, 139-140; waste of, 143-144

Lend Lease, 171, 172, 176, 178

Lenin, Vladimir Ilyich, 167

Lewis, Sinclair, 128

Lincoln, Abraham, x, 31, 54, 63, 81, 90, 121; Emerson's view of, 24; as typical hero, 24-27; his belief in man, 57; Theodore Roosevelt's view of, 105; and Truman, 119

Lippmann, Walter, 144

Lloyd, Henry Demarest, 58, 74

Louisiana Purchase, 8, 11

McCarthyites, 182

McKinley, William, 54-55, 63

Marshall, George, 179

Marx, Karl, 64

Meat industry, 32

Mellon, Thomas, 41, 45

Mexico, 16, 160-161, 168-169

Minorities: under New Deal, 115-116

Monroe Doctrine, 17, 158

Morgan, J. Pierpont, 38, 43, 46

Morgenthau, Henry, 88

National Youth Administration, 135

Negroes: and Emerson, 24; gifts for education of, 73; middle class, 91-92; and segregation in Washington, 109; and New Deal, 116; and Truman, 119-120; and success, 138

New Deal, 113-118; and right to work, 134-136

New Frontier: and culture, 146-147

Nixon, Richard, 183

North Atlantic Treaty Organization, 180

Occupational status: early 20th century, 67-68

Oil industry, 32, 33

Organization for European Economic Cooperation, 179

Organization of American States, 185, 188

Outlook, 71

Panama, 158, 168

Philippines, 154, 157, 159, 160, 166

Plunkitt, George Washington, 82-83

Poland, 16

Politics: and Jefferson, 8; and farmers, 98-99; and labor, 99-100; and social reform, 100-103; in 20th century, 100-104; moderation in, 119, 120

Poor Richard's Almanac, 5

Populism, 55

Potsdam, 176
Prejudice, ethnic, 66, 88-89
President's Commission on Civil Rights, 119-120
Puerto Rico, 154
Pullman strike, 56

Radicalism: early 20th century, 89-90
Railroads, 32, 33, 35
Republican Party: in the 1920's, 111
Rhee, Syngman, 181, 186
Rockefeller, John D., 36, 43
Rockefeller, John D., Jr., 93
Rockefeller Foundation, 78
Roosevelt, Franklin, 120, 134, 186, 188; and the New Deal, 113-117; and foreign policy, 168-177
Roosevelt, Theodore, 81, 88, 93, 112, 120; his opinion of William McKinley, 55; as example of the middle class, 74-75, 76, 77; predicts Catholic will become President, 82; as President, 105-107; and Franklin Roosevelt, 113, 168; on work, 125-126; foreign policy of, 155-160
Russia: and Theodore Roosevelt, 156; and Woodrow Wilson, 164; and Franklin Roosevelt, 169, 174-177; and Truman, 178; and Eisenhower, 182; and Cuba, 185; after Cuban crisis, 186-187
Ryan, Father John, 81

St. Nicholas, 71
Salt, Albert, 127-128, 129, 131
Santo Domingo, 158
Saturday Evening Post, The, 46, 69, 71, 89; its "Men and Women of the Hour," 66-68

Scandinavian-Americans, 87
Sherman Antitrust Act, 52, 102, 106
Sloan, Alfred, 130
Smith, Adam, 39
Smith, Alfred E., 86-87, 88
Social conditions: early 20th century, 65-66
Social status: early 20th century, 68-69; anxiety about, 73-74
Social work: and political reform, 100-103
Socialist Labor Party, 90
South Korea, 186
Soviet Union. See Russia
Spanish-American War, 154
Spencer, Herbert, 39, 41
Square Deal, 106, 114
Stalin, Joseph, 174, 175
Standard of living: as gauge of esteem, 131
Steel industry, 32, 33
Straus, Isadore, 88
Straus, Nathan, 88
Straus, Oscar, 88
Style, 138-139, 142
Suez crisis, 182
Sullivan, John L., 83

Taft, William Howard: as President, 107-108; foreign policy of, 160
Taxes. See Income tax
Taylor, Frederick Winslow, 126
Telegraph, 32
Telephone, 32
Textile industry, 32, 33
Truman, Harry S, 186; domestic policies of, 119-120; foreign policy of, 178-181; and Latin America, 183
Tumulty, Joseph Patrick, 84-87, 88, 93

Turkey, 178

United Nations, 176, 180, 182, 188, 189

United Nations Relief and Rehabilitation Administration, 176

U. S. Constitution, 11, 54; and Fourteenth Amendment, 50, 51-52

U. S. Department of Agriculture, 78

U. S. Steel Corporation, 37

U. S. Supreme Court: and corporations, 50-54; and New Deal, 116

Vanderlip, Frank Arthur, 70

Veblen, Thorstein, 126, 138

Venezuela, 157

Versailles, Treaty of, 166

Vietnam, 186, 187

Virginia, 8

Washington, Booker T., 91-92, 105

Washington, George, 17, 54, 56; Hamilton aide to, 10; as symbol of patriotism, 14-15; and Lincoln, 25

Waste: and American abundance, 130

Weems, Parson, 14

Whitehead, Alfred North, 142, 148

Who's Who in America, 68

Wilson, Woodrow, 88, 112, 113, 168; and Tumulty, 86; domestic policies of, 108-110; foreign policy of, 160-166

Work: as a virtue, 125-126, 133-134; and advertising, 131; under New Deal, 134-136

World Bank, 176

World War I, 162-164

World War II, 173-175

Yalta, 174-175

Youth's Companion, 71